An Historical List, Of All Horse-matches Run, By J. Cheny

Anonymous

h

101.

AN
Hiſtorical LIST
OF ALL
Horſe-Matches Run,

And of all

PLATES and PRIZES Run for in *England* and *Wales* (of the Value of Ten Pounds or upwards) in 1731.

CONTAINING

The Names of the Owners of the HORSES that have Run as above, and the Names and Colours of the ſaid HORSES alſo.

WITH

The Winner diſtinguiſhed of every MATCH, PLATE, PRIZE, or STAKES: The Conditions of Running, as to Weight, Age, Size, &c. and the Places in which the loſing HORSES have come in.

With a LIST alſo of the Principal COCK-MATCHES of the Year above, and who were the Winners and Loſers of them, &c.

By JOHN CHENY.

LONDON: Printed in the Year M.DCC.XXXI.

AN

Hiſtorical LIST

OF

Horſe-Matches, &c.

NEWMARKET, 1731.

HE Royal Prizes of the Kingdom, in the preſent Year, have been fourteen in number, thirteen of which were Preſents from the Crown; conſiſting, as in preceding Years, of an hundred Guineas each in Specie, and run for at the ſame Places as in 1730: and the fourteenth of the ſame was a Preſent of His Royal Highneſs the Prinee to the City of *Coventry*. To which fourteen in *England*, is again added a Liſt of *Edinburgh*, advancing the Royal Prizes of this Book to the number of fifteen.

A 2   And

And becauſe the Method continues of run-ning for the firſt of the ſame at *Newmarket*, I di-rectly proceed to a Liſt of *Newmarket*; where the firſt Sport of the Year was a Match, run on the 31ſt Day of *March*, between the Earl of *Portmore's Victorious*, and the Duke of *Bolton's Gypſy*; 8 *ſt.* 4 *m.* 300 Guineas; which Match was won by *Victorious*.

On the ſame Day, the Earl of *Portmore's Daffidil* beat Mr. *Coke's Silver-Locks*; 8 *ſt.* 4 *m.* 200 Guineas.

On the 1ſt Day of *April*, the firſt Royal Prize of the Year was run for here; conſiſting, as obſerv'd, of 100 Guineas, and being free for ſix Year Olds only, carrying 12 *ſt.*

	1 H.	2 H.	3 H.
This Prize was won by the Earl of *Godolphin's* Black H. *Morrat*, bred by Sir *William Ramſden*, and got by *Bay Bolton* ———— ———— ————	1	2	1
Earl of *Portmore's* Grey H. *Craftſ-man*, got by *Smiling Tom* ———	3	1	2
Mr. *Sheppard's* Cheſ. H. *Tarran* ———	2	3	3

3d *ditto*, Sir *Michael Newton's* Cheſ. M. *Bridget*, got by *Bloody-Buttocks*, beat the Duke of *Bolton's* Bay H. *Jackanapes*, got by *Jigg*; 8 *ſt.* 7 *l.* 4 *m.* 200 Guineas.

On the 5th *ditto*, the following three ſtarted for a Purſe of 400 Guineas, *wt.* 10 *ſt.* one four Miles Heat.

	1 H.
Lord *Gower's* Bay M. *Diana*, got by *Cyprus* ————	1
Duke of *Devonſhire's Polly*, got by *Childers* ————	2
Duke of *Bridgewater's Traveller* ———	3

7th

7th *ditto*, Duke of *Ancaster*'s Chef. *Filly*, beat Sir *Robert Fagg*'s Chef. *Filly*; 8 *ft.* the lowest give and take, 4 *m.* 200 Guineas.

On the 10th *ditto*, the fecond Royal Prize of the Year was run for here, free only for five Year old Mares; *wt.* 10 *ft.* one four Miles Heat:

	H.
which Prize was won by Mr. *Jackson*'s Grey M. *Favourite*, bred as in my laft, *page* 18.	1
Duke of *Bolton*'s Black M. *Gypfey*, bred by Sir *William Ramfden*, got by *Bay-Bolton*	2
Earl of *Haverfham*'s Chef. M. *Mifs Sally*, got by *Hartly*'s Blind-Horfe	3
Duke of *Rutland*'s Grey M. got by *Hall*'s *Arabian*	4

20th *ditto*, Mr. *Hals*'s Bay G. *Quid-Nunc*, 7 *ft.* beat Lord *St. John*'s Dun G. 6 *ft.* 4 *m.* 100 Guineas.

21ft *ditto*, Earl of *Portmore*'s *Victorious*, 8 *ft.* 8 *l.* beat the Duke of *Bridgewater*'s *Star*, 8. *ft.* 5 *l.* 4 *m.* 300 Guineas.

On the 23d *ditto*, the following four Year Olds ftarted for a Purfe of 800 Guineas, being the fecond of the five Years Subfcription, *wt.* 8 *ft.* 7 *l.* one four Miles Heat.

	H.
Sir *Michael Newton*'s Grey H. *Loufe*, got by *Bloody-Buttocks*	1
Duke of *Somerfet*'s Bay H. bred by Mr. *Sheppard*	2
Duke of *Devonfhire*'s Bay H. *Comical*, got by *Childers*	3
Duke of *Bolton*'s Bay H. *Jeffamin-Tom*, got by *Bay-Bolton*	4

Lord

Lord Viſcount *Londſdale*'s Grey H. *Waſp,* }
   got by his Lordſhip's *Arabian,* —— } H. 5

Earl of *Godolphin*'s Bay H. *Bobtail* —— | 6

24th *ditto;* Mr. *Tuting*'s *Cynder-Wench* beat Mr. *Harriſon*'s *Strickland;* 10 ſt. 6 m. 100 Guineas.

27th *ditto,* Earl of *Portmore*'s *Hutton,* beat the Duke of *Bridgewater*'s *Nathan;* 8 ſt. 4 l. 4 m. 300 Guineas.

Same Day Mr. *Warren*'s Bay Horſe, beat Sir *Herbert Packington*'s Bay M. 10 ſt. 2 m. 100 Guineas.

On the following Day, the ſame Horſe of Mr. *Warren*'s beat the ſame Mare of Sir *Herbert Packington*'s; 10 ſt. 2 m. 100 Guineas.

Same Day Earl of *Portmore*'s *Daffidil,* 9 ſt. beat Mr. *Cornewall*'s *Poſt-Boy,* 8 ſt. 4 m. 100 Guineas.

29th *ditto,* Mr. *Coke*'s *Silver-Locks* beat Mr. *Piearſe*'s *Smugler,* 8 ſt. 6 m. 200 Guineas.

On the 1ſt of *May,* Mr. *South*'s *Duſty-Miller,* beat Mr. *Adams*'s *Cinnamon,* 9 ſt. 4 m. 10 Guineas.

30th *ditto,* Mr. *Adams*'s *Cynder-Wench,* beat Mr. *South*'s *Duſty-Miller,* 9 ſt. 4 m. 10 Guineas; which Match concluded the Sport at this Place in the Spring: After which, the firſt Sport that ſucceeded, was a Prize of 80 Guineas, run for on the 5th of *October,* by the following three, *wt.* 9 ſt. one Heat.

Duke of *Ancaſter*'s Grey H. *Crab* —— | H. 1

Lord *Gower*'s Bay *Filly* —— | 2

Duke of *Bridgewater*'s *Robin* —— | 3

On the following Day, the Duke of *Devonſhire*'s *Scar* beat the Duke of *Bolton*'s *Fear-not,* 8 ſt. 7 l. 4 m. 500 Guineas.

Same Day, Earl of *Portmore*'s *Childers,* beat the Duke of *Bridgewater*'s *Nathan;* 8 ſt. 4 l. 4 m. 300 Guineas.

On

On the 7th *ditto*, the three following started for the 13th and last hundred Royal Guineas of the Year in *England*; free only for 6 Year Olds, *wt.* 12 *st.*

	H.	H.
Mr. *Jackson*'s Grey M. *Favourite* ——	1	1
Duke of *Somerset*'s Grey H. *Grey-Legs*	2	2
Sir *Nathaniel Curzon*'s Grey H. *Brisk*, lamed and distanced ——	3	*dis*

8th *ditto*, Duke of *Devonshire*'s *Comical*, beat the Duke of *Bolton*'s *Younker*; 8 *st.* 5 *l.* 4 *m.* 300 Guin.

Same Day, Mr. *Cotton*'s *Commoner*, beat Mr. *Henly*'s Bay Colt; 8 *st.* 2 *l.* 4 *m.* 200 Guineas.

9th *ditto*, Duke of *Bridgewater*'s *Hazard*, beat Lord *Gower*'s *Fielding*; 8 *st.* 8 *l.* 4 *m.* 200 Guineas.

14th *ditto*, Mr. *Robinson*'s Chef. M. started alone for the Town-Plate of 20 Guineas Value; *wt.* 12 *st.*

The following four, *viz.*

Duke of *Bolton*'s *Bess-a-Bell*,
Earl of *Portmore*'s *Fox*,
Mr. *Coke*'s *Bauble*, and
Mr. *Cotton*'s *Commoner*,

were matched to run on the 25th *ditto*, for 200 Guineas each, half Forfeit, *wt.* 8 *st.* 5 *l.* one four Miles Heat; but *Bess-a-Bell* and *Fox* paid Forfeit, which reduced the Prize from 800 Guineas to 600; which six hundred were run for on the aforesaid Day by *Commoner* and *Bauble*, and won by *Commoner*. *Commoner* was got by the Duke of *Devonshire*'s *Childers*, and *Bauble* by the bald Galloway.

On the 26th *ditto*, the following five Year Olds started for the Stakes, consisting of 180 Guineas; *wt.* 9 *st.* one four Miles Heat.

	H.
Earl of *Hallifax*'s Bay H. got by *Jigg* ——	1
Duke of *Devonshire*'s Chef. H. got by *Childers* ——	2

Duke

	H.
Duke of *Somerset*'s Bay H. ————	3
Earl of *Portmore*'s Bay H. got by Lord *Lonsdale*'s *Arabian* —————	4
Sir *Michael Newton*'s Grey G. got by *Bloody-Buttocks* —————	5
Duke of *Bolton*'s Bay H. *Jessamin-Tom*—	6

Same Day, Sir *Michael Newton*'s *Louse* beat the Duke of *Ancaster*'s *Crab*; 10 *ft.* 4 *m.* 200 Guineas.

27th *ditto*, Mr. *Panton*'s *Mouse*, got by *Childers*, beat the Duke of *Bolton*'s *Jackanapes*; 8 *ft.* 5 *l.* 4 *m.* 300 Guineas.

Same Day, Mr. *Cornewall*'s Chef. H. *Post-Boy*, got by *Old Post-Boy*, 8 *ft.* beat Earl of *Portmore*'s *Childers*, 9 *ft.* 4 *m.* 500 Guineas.

28th *ditto*, Mr. *Coke*'s *Silver-Locks*, 7 *ft.* 7 *l.* beat the Earl of *Portmore*'s *Daffidil*, 8 *ft.* 4 *m.* 300 Guin.

On the 1ft Day of *November*; Earl of *Portmore*'s *Victorious*, beat Mr. *Fleetwood*'s *Fox-Hunter*, 8 *ft.* 7 *l.* 4 *m.* 50 Guineas.

2d *ditto*, Mr. *Bromley*'s Galloway beat Mr. *Cornewall*'s Hunter, 8 *ft.* 7 *l.* 4 *m.* 100 Guineas.

Same Day, Mr. *Hawkins*'s Galloway, beat Mr. *Bromley*'s Galloway, 8 *ft.* 7 *l.* 4 *m.* 10 Guineas; which Match concluded the Sport at this Place for the Year.

WIN-

✿✿✿✿✿✿✿✿✿✿✿✿✿✿✿✿✿

WINCHESTER, 1731.

THE third Royal Prize of the Year, was that of *Winchester*, run for on the 18th Day of *May*; and being as usual, for six Year Olds, carrying 12 *st.* entering for the same the Day before running.

	1 H.
This Prize was won by	
Mr. *Jackson*'s Grey M. *Favourite*————	1
Mr. *Garrard*'s Chef. H. *Trooper*————	dis
Mr. *Orm*'s Chef. H. fell, and broke } from his Rider ———————— }	dis
Mr. *Beacon*'s Chef. H. took the rest——	dis

On the following Day, upon this Course, a 20 *l.* Plate was run for, free only for such as never won 50 *l. wt.* 10 *st.* and won by

	1 H.	2 H.
Mr. *Coles*'s Grey M. *Painted-Lady*——	1	1
Mr. *Worsley*'s Chef. H. *Smiling-Ball*——	2	2
A Hack to Quality———————	dis	

A third Prize of this Meeting, was a 20 *l.* Plate for Galloways, 9 *st.* the highest give and take; and won by

	1 H.	
Sir *Arthur Haslerige*'s Bay M. *Sweet-* } *Maidenhead* ———————— }	1	
Mr. *Coles*'s Black G. *Little-Esquire* ——	2	
Mr. *Try*'s Chef. M. 13 H. 3 I. ¼.———	dis	

The

The fourth and laſt Prize of this Meeting, was a Purſe of 40 Guineas, for ſuch as never won a Royal Plate; *wt.* 11 *ſt.* and won by

	1 H.	2 H.
Mr. *Green*'s Cheſ. H. *Merry-Andrew*	1	1
Sir *Arthur Haſlerige*'s Cheſ. G. *Robin-Red-Breaſt*	2	2
Mr. *Sheppard*'s Brown H. *Brown-Darcy*	3	3

SALIS-

SALISBURY, 1731.

ON the 1st Day of *June*, the fourth King's Plate of the Year was run for at *Salisbury*, consisting of 100 Guineas, for six Year Olds, *wt.* 12 *st.* and won by

	H.
Mr. *Jackson*'s Grey M. *Favourite*————	1
Mr. *Orm*'s Chef. H. lamed and distanced	*dis*
Mr. *Ince*'s Grey M. ————————	*dis*

Upon this Course, the following Day, a 20 Guin. Purse was run for, free only for such as never won 50 Guineas; *wt.* 11 *st.* to enter seven Days before, paying one Guinea or two at the Post.

	H.
This Prize was won by	
Mr. *Orm*'s Chef. G. *Fidler* ————	1
Mr. *Fownes*'s Chef. G. ————————	*dis*
Mr. *Monk*'s Chef. G. ————————	*dis*

On the 3d *ditto*, upon this Course, a 20 *l.* Plate was run for, *wt.* 10 *st.* to enter seven Days before, paying one Guinea or two at the Post: Stakes for the second best.

	H.
This Prize was won by	
Mr. *Harvey*'s Bay H. *Fiddler*————	1
Mr. *Willis*'s Grey M. *Miss Dove*————	2
Mr. *Orm*'s Chef. G. *Fiddler*, lamed ——	*dis*

GUILD-

GUILDFORD, 1731.

THE fifth Royal Prize of the Year, was the 100 Guineas at *Guildford*, run for on the 8th of *June*, on the usual Conditions, being for six Year Olds, carrying 12 *st.*

	1 H.	2 H.	3 H.
This Prize was won by the Duke of *Somerset*'s Grey H. *Grey-Legs*, bred by His Grace——	1	3	1
Mr. *Banks*'s Ches. H. *Bald Fox-hunter*, bred by the Duke of *Ancaster*——	2	1	2
Earl of *Portmore*'s Black G. *Jack-daw*, got by *Hipp*——	3	2	dr.
Mr. *Beacon*'s Ches. H. *Foxhunter*——	4	dr.	
Mr. *Fortescue*'s Grey H. *Leopard*——	dis		

On the 9th *ditto*, on the same Course, was 20 *l.* Plate for Galloways, 9 *st.* the highest give and take; and won by

	1 H.	2 H.
Mr. *Rich*'s Grey H. *Harlequin* ——	1	1
Mr. *Henly*'s Bay H. *Pebble-Stone*——	2	2

On the following Day, on this Course, the 50 *l.* Plate was run for, free only for such as never won a Royal Prize, *wt.* 10 *st.*

This

	1 H.	2 H.
This Prize was won by		
Mr. *Green*'s Chef. H. *Merry-Andrew*, often call'd *Salisbury-Steeple*	1	1
Earl of *Portmore*'s Grey H. *Craftsman* ———	2	2
Mr. *Trewet*'s Brown H. *Merry-Tom* fell, and threw his Rider just after starting ———	*dif*	

Enter for all three, *Monday* before running, paying for the 20*l*. Plate one Guinea, for the 50*l*. Plate three Guineas.

B

Ipswich, 1731.

ON the 15th Day of *June*, the fixth Royal Prize of the Year was run for at *Ipſwich*; conſiſting, as obſerv'd, of 100 Guineas, and being free for five Year Olds only; *wt.* 10 *ſt.* 2 Miles at a Heat.

This Prize was won by	1H.	2H.	3H.
Mr. *Dodſworth*'s Grey H. *Midge*, bred by himſelf ————	3	1	1
Earl of *Hallifax*'s Grey H. *Sore-Heels*, bred by Mr. *Croft*, and got by *Sore-Heels*————	1	3	3
Mr. *Jackſon*'s Grey H. *Grizle*, bred by himſelf, and got by Mr. *Bridge-water*'s Horſe ————	2	2	2
Sir *Robert Fagg*'s Grey H. *Fox*, bred by the Rev^d. Mr. *Carter*, and got by *Fox* ————	4	4	4
Mr. *Fauquier*'s Grey H. *Nutmeg*, bred by Mr. *Atkinſon* ————	5	dr.	
Duke of *Somerſet*'s Grey H. *Grey Sheppard*, bred by Mr. *Sheppard*———	diſ		
Hon. Mr. *Bertie*'s Grey G. *Snap*, bred by himſelf ———	diſ		
Mr. *Peck*'s Bay H. *Brown-George*, bred by Major *Gipps*———	diſ		
Mr. *Johnſon*'s Cheſ. H. *Ambaſſador*, bred by himſelf ————	diſ		

On the following Day, upon this Courſe, a 30 Guineas Purſe was run for, free only for ſuch Galloways as never won 100 Guineas; 9 *ſt.* the higheſt
give

give and take: to enter the Day before, paying half a Guinea.

	1H.	
This Prize was won by Sir *Arthur Haflerige*'s Bay M. *Ring-Tail*; 13 H. 2 I. ¼.	1	
Duke of *Somerfet*'s Brown M. 13 H. 2 I. ½.	*dif*	

On the 17th *ditto*, upon the fame Courfe, a Plate of 25 *l*. Value was run for, free only for Hunters within 15 Miles of *Ipfwich*; *wt*. 11 *ft*. and won by

	1H.	2H.	3H.
Mr. *Baines*'s Bay G. *Bobtail*	2	1	1
Mr. *Hale*'s Bay G. *Small-Hopes*	1	2	3
Mr. *Elfden*'s Chef. M. *Weafel*	3	3	2
Mr. *Matthews*'s Brown G. *Ramper*	*dif*		
Mr. *Woodthorp*'s Grey G. *Midge*	*dif*		

NOTE

NOTTINGHAM, 1731.

ON the 5th Day of *July*, the seventh Hundred Royal Guineas of the Year were run for at *Nottingham*, being for six Year Olds; *wt.* 12 *st.* and won by

	1 H.	2 H.	3 H.
Mr. *Rich*'s Bay H. *Lowther*, bred by the late Sir *W. Lowther*, and got by *Snake*	1	3	1
Mr. *Hutton*'s Bay H. *Black-Legs*	4	1	2
Mr. *Taylor*'s Brown H. *Fear-not*	5	2	3
Mr. *Rawlinson*'s Brown H. *Whittington*, lamed	2	dr.	
Mr. *Jackson*'s Grey M. *Favourite*	3	dr.	
Mr. *Rickaby*'s Black M. *Patch-Buttocks*	6	dr.	

On the following Day, on this Course, the Ladies Plate was run for; consisting of a Purse of 50 Guin. free only for such Hunters as had been at the death of ten Brace of Hares, and one Brace of Foxes, in the preceding Season, and had not been in Sweats from the 1st Day of *November* last past, and the last Day of *March*, and that had not won a Plate since the first of the past *October*; enter *Saturday* before, paying 5 Guineas, *wt.* 14 *st.* and rode by such Gentlemen as never rode among Grooms. Had but one enter'd for this Prize, to be allow'd 10 Guineas and Charges, and the said Prize not to be run for; but there started for the same the five following.

Lord

✠✠✠✠✠✠✠✠✠✠✠✠✠✠✠✠✠✠✠✠✠✠✠✠

CANTERBURY, 1731.

ON the 11th of *January*, at *Canterbury*, Mr. *Arnold*'s Bay G. *Creeping-Dick*, beat Mr. *Toker*'s Bay M. beft of three Heats, 8 *ſt*. 20 Guineas.

On the fame Courſe the following Day, Mr. *Croſier*'s Cheſ. H. *Cupid* beat Mr. *Arnold*'s Cheſ. H. 8 *ſt*. 4 *m*. 10 Guineas.

On the fame Courſe, on the 15th *ditto*, Mr. *Croſier*'s *Cupid* beat Mr. *Arnold*'s Bay G. *Creeping Dick*, beft of three Heats, 8 *ſt*. 20 Guineas.

On the fame Courſe, on the 6th of *April*, Mr. *Croſier*'s *Cupid* beat Mr. *Arnold*'s *Creeping-Dick*, beft alſo of three Heats, 8 *ſt*. 20 Guineas.

Upon *Eaſter Tueſday*, upon this Courſe, a 10 *l*. Plate was run for, *wt*. 10 *ſt*. excluſive of Bridle and Saddle, one Heat.

	H. 1
This Prize was won by	
Mr. *Selby*'s Brown H. *Swallow*———	1
Mr. *Moore*'s Grey M. *Smiling-Kate* ———	2
Mr. *Woodman*'s Grey H. *Gander*———	3
Mr. *Harvy*'s Grey G. *Bonny George*———	4
Sir *Tho. Hale*'s Grey M. *Miſs Maggot*—	5
Mr. *Laſington*'s Brown G. *Foxhunter*—	6
Mr. *Spence*'s Black G. *Chimney-Sweeper*	7

In the latter end of *April*, upon this Courſe, Mr. *Croſier*'s *Cupid*, beat Mr. *Arnold*'s Grey M. 8 *ſt*. beft of three Heats, 4 *m*. 20 Guineas.

On the 19th of *May*, on the ſame Courſe, Mr. *Croſier*'s Bay M. beat Mr. *Arnold*'s *Creeping-Dick*, beft of three Heats, 8 *ſt*. 20 Guineas.

On

On the 10th Day of *August*, the 9th King's Plate of the Year was run for upon this Course, confisting of an 100 Guineas, for 6 Year Olds, *wt.* 12 *ft.* and won by

	1 H.	2 H.
Sir *George Oxendon's* Chef. M.———	1	1
Mr. *Glanvill's* Chef. H. *Spot* ———	2	2
Mr. *Moore's* Grey M. *Smiling Kate*——	3	3
Mr. *Badcock's* Grey G. *Why-not* ———	dif	

On the fame Course, the following Day, a Purfe of 60 Guineas was run for, free only for fuch as had three Months before been the Property of a Subfcriber to this Prize, *wt.* 12 *ft.* 50 of which Guineas to be the Prize of the firft Horfe, and the other 10 as Stakes, the Property of the 2d. There ftarted for this Cafh the two following

	1 H.	2 H.
Mr. *Fagg's* Grey H. *Merry Jack*———	1	1
Mr. *Curtis's* Bay G.———————	2	dif

This Gelding of Mr. *Curtis's* was not diftanced in Running, but the Rider in the 2d Heat omitted to prove his Weight; in Default of which, the 10 Guineas, affign'd for the 2d beft, was given to the firft, and the s^d Gelding deem'd diftanc'd.

On the 12th *ditto*, on the fame Course, a Purfe of 15 Guineas was run for, free only for fuch Galloways as never won above 30 Guineas, 9 *ft.* the higheft give and take; and won by

	1 H.	2 H.
Mr. *Crofier's* Bay M. 13 H. 2 I. $\frac{1}{4}$ ———	1	1
Mr. *Oldfworth's* Bay G. *Creeping Dick*, 13 H. 2 I. —————	2	2
Mr. *Crofier's* Cupid, 14 H. ———	3	3

On

On the fame Courfe, on the 13th *ditto*, a Purfe of 20 Guineas was run for, free only for fuch as never won 40 Guineas, *wt.* 12 *ft.* and the Winner to be fold for 40 Guineas.

This Prize was won by
Mr. *Moore's* Grey M. *Smiling Kate* ————
Mr. *Clark's* Brown H. *Fear-not* ————

	1 H.	2 H.
	1	1
	2	C

On the fame Courfe, on the 24th of *September*, Mr. *Crofier's* Bay M. beat Mr. *Oldfworth's* Bay G. beft of 3 Heats, 8 *ft.* 20 Guineas.

BLACK-

BLACK-HAMBLETON. 1731.

ON the 13th Day of *August*, the 20 Guineas for 4 Year Olds, *wt.* 10 *st.* one 3 Miles Heat, were run for at *Hambleton*, and won by

	H.
The Duke of *Bolton*'s Grey H. got by Bay *Bolton* ———	1
Mr. *Dalton*'s Grey H. got by Lord *Lonsdale*'s *Arabian* ———	2
Mr. *Sanderson*'s Grey M. got by Commoner ———	3
Mr. *Curbutson*'s Chef. M. got by *Castaway* ———	4
Mr. *White*'s Bay H. got by *Bell*'s Horse ———	5
Mr. *Benson*'s Bay H. got by *Aleppo* —	6
Lord Viscount *Lonsdale*'s Grey H. got by the Grey *Turk* ———	7
Mr. *Berry*'s Bay H. ———	8
Mr. *Pullen*'s Bay H. got by *Figg* ———	9
Mr. *Metcalf*'s Chef. H. got by the Grey *Arabian* at *Hampton-Court*	10
Sir *John Stapleton*'s Grey M. got by *Aleppo* ———	11
Mr. *Cornforth*'s M. got by *Bell*'s Horse	12
Mr. *Delavall*'s Chef. H. got by *Hartly*'s Blind Horse ———	13
Mr. *Wilkinson*'s Bay ———	14
Mr. *Rakes*'s Bay M. got by *Young Childers* ———	15

On

On the following Day, on the fame Courfe, the King's 100 Guineas, for 5 Year Old Mares, were run for, *wt.* 10 *st.* one four Miles Heat.

	H.
Which Prize was won by	
The Duke of *Bolton*'s Grey, got by *Almanzor*	1
Mr. *Spinks*'s Dun, got by *Johnson's Turk*	2
Mr. *Williams*'s Bay, got by Mr. *Williams Wynn*'s *Arabian*	3
Mr. *Deighton*'s Grey, got by *Aleppo*	4
Mr. *Tims*'s Chef.	5
Mr. *Dutchet*'s Chef. got by *Bawtry*'s Blind Horfe	6
Mr. *Soulsby*'s Grey, got by *Hipp*	7
Mr. *Robinson*'s Grey, got by *Spark*	8
Mr. *Henry*'s Brown, got by *Tarran*'s Barb	9
Mr. *Watson*'s Bay, got by *Fox*	10
Mr. *Wright*'s Bay, got by *Bell*'s Horfe	11
Mr. *Gregg*'s Grey	12
Mr. *Wilson*'s Chef. got by *Young Childers*	13
Mr. *Grimes*'s Bay, got by *Almanzor*	14
Mr. *Metcalf*'s Chef. got by the bald Galloway	15
Mr. *Aislabie*'s Chef. got by the bald Galloway	16
Mr. *Erret*'s Bay, got by *Flower*	17
Mr. *Creswell*'s Grey, got by *Hipp*	18
Mr. *Knowles*'s Bay, got by *Skip-Jack*	19
Mr. *Laking*'s Chef. got by *Johnson*'s Turk	20
Mr. *Grimes*'s Black, got by *Champion*	21
Mr. *Routh*'s Chef. got by *Hutton*'s White-Hunter	22
Mr. *Colvil*'s Bay, got by a Son of *Darlow*'s *Arabian*	23

C

YORK, 1731.

THE 11th King's Plate of the Year was the 100 Guineas at *York*, run for on the 16th Day of *August*, being for 6 Year Olds, carrying 12 *ft*. which Prize was won by the Lord Viscount *Lonsdale*'s Bay H. *Monkey*, bred by himself, and got by a Foreign Horse of his Lordship's, and being also the same that won the great Stakes of 800 Guineas at *Newmarket* in *April* 1730.

	1 H.	2 H.
He came ———	1	1
Sir *Nathaniel Curzon*'s Grey H. *Brisk*, got by the Bloody-Shoulder'd *Arabian* ———	4	2
Mr. *Benson*'s Bay H. *Johnson*, got by *Johnson*'s Turk ———	2	dr.
Mr. *Vavasor*'s Chef. H. *Mercury*, got by *Almanzor* ———	3	dif
Mr. *Dawson*'s Grey H. *True-blue* —	dif	
Mr. *Taylor*'s Brown H. *Bay Buster*, got by *Champion* ———	dif	
Mr. *Cooper*'s Chef. M. *Now-or-never*	dif	

A 2d Prize of this Meeting was a 30 *l.* Purse, on the 17th *ditto*, *wt.* 11 *ft.* Stakes 3 Guineas, which Prize was won by

	1 H.	2 H.
Mr. *Brewster*'s Bay M. *Miss Nesham*	1	1
Mr. *Bathurst*'s Grey H. *Merry Quaker*	3	2

Sir

	1 H.	2 H.
Sir *Marmaduke Wyvill*'s Black H. } *Scarborough Colt* ——— —— }	2	3

On the 18th *ult.* on the fame Courfe, a Purfe of 40 *l.* Sterling was run for, free only for 6 Year Olds, *wt.* 10 *ft.* Stakes 8 Guineas, and won by

	1 H.	2 H.	3 H.
Mr. *Benfon*'s Bay H. *Johnfon* ———	2	1	1
Mr. *Smith*'s Bay M. *Smiling Molly* ——	1	3	4
Mr. *Mountain*'s Grey H. *Fear not* } got by *Aleppo* ——— }	3	2	2
Revd. Mr. *Tarran*'s Bay H. *Barb* } got by his Black *Barb* ——— }	4	4	3

On the following Day, on the fame Courfe, a Purfe of 60 *l.* Sterling was run for, free only for 5 Year Olds, carrying 10 *ft.* one Heat, Stakes 15 Guineas. This Prize was won by

	1 H.
Mr. *Lifter*'s Grey H. *Dunkirk*, got } by the *Fox Cubb* ——— }	1
Mr. *Bathurft*'s Chef. H. *Freeman* } of *York* ——— }	2
Mr. *Fletcher*'s Bay H. *Prince Pretty*, } got by *Young Childers* ——— }	3
Mr. *Thompfon*'s Bay H. *Carelefs* got } by *Fox* ——— }	4
Mr. *Smales*'s Bay H. *Smales Childers* } got by *Young Childers* ——— }	5
Mr. *Aiflabie*'s Chef. H. *Better-Luck*, } got by *Figg* ——— }	6
Mr. *Humberftone*'s Grey H. *Blue-Ribbon*, got by *Alcock*'s Horfe ——— }	7

C 2

Mr.

	1 H.
Mr. *Twizle*'s Grey H. *Quiet Cuddy*, got by *Hipp* ———	8
Mr. *Wharton*'s Bay H. *Single-Peeper*, got by *Fox* ———	9
Mr. *Bacchus*'s Grey H. *Greyhound*, got by *Smiling Tom* ———	10
Lord Viscount *Lonsdale*'s Chef. H. *Surly*, got by the *Curwen* Colt at *Hampton-Court* ———	11
Mr. *Fenwick*'s Brown H. *Young Swallow*———	12
Mr. *Anderson*'s Brown H. *Positive*, got by a Son of *Curwen*'s Bay *Barb*; he did not come in to prove his Weight ———	

Upon this Course, on the 20th *ditto*, was a 20 *l.* Purse, for Galloways, 9 *st.* the highest give and take, Stakes 3 Guineas; which Prize was won by

	1 H.	2 H.	3 H.
Mr. *Dixon*'s Bay H. *Smiling Joke*, 13 H. 2 I. ¾ ———	4	1	1
Mr. *Hedley*'s Bay M. *Now-or-never*, 13 H. 3 I. ¼ ———	1	2	2
Mr. *White*'s Bay M. *Sweetlips*, 13 H. ¼ I. ———	2	dif	
Mr. *Munday*'s Grey H. *Hopeful*, 14 H.	3	dif	

The last Prize of this Meeting was a Purse of 25 Guineas, *wt.* 12 *st.* and rode for by Gentlemen, Stakes 5 Guineas.

	1 H.	2 H.
This Prize was won by Capt. *Gee*'s Bay H. *Fox-Hunter* ———	1	1

Mr.

	1 H.	2 H.	3 H.
Mr. *Brewster's* Chef. H. *Hark away*	3	3	2
Mr. *Bathurst's* Grey A. *Merry Qua-ker* ——————— ——— }	2	2	2
Mr. *Thorold's* Chef. M. *Diana* ———	dif		
Mr. *Kilvington's* Bay M. *Caft-away*	dif		

LINCOLN, 1731.

ON the 6th Day of *September*, the 12th 100 Royal Guineas of the Year were run for at *Lincoln*, free for 6 Year Olds, carrying 12 *st*. Which Prize was won by

	1 H.	2 H.	3 H.
Sir *Nathaniel Curzon*'s Grey H. *Brisk*	3	1	1
Mr. *Jackson*'s Grey M. *Favourite* ——	1	5	2
Mr. *Rawlinson*'s Chef. H. *Turn-a-gain Whittington* ——————	5	2	dif
Earl of *Hallifax*'s Chef. H. *Juftice*—	6	3	dr.
Mr. *Rickaby*'s Black M. *Patch-Buttocks*	2	4	dr.
Mr. *White*'s Grey M. *Miss Brigham*——	4	dif	
Duke of *Bridgewater*'s Chef. H. *Traveller* —————	7	dif	
Lord *Onflow*'s Bay H. *Crifpin* ———	dif		
Mr. *Bacon*'s Chef. H. *Tickle her Whim* —————	dif		
Mr. *Townrow*'s Grey H. *Spot* —————	dif		

On the 7th *ditto*, on the fame Courfe, a 20 *l.* Plate was run for, free only for fuch as never won above 20 *l.* 14 Hands, to carry 9 *st.* and to give or take if higher or lower; 3 to ftart, and a five Pound Plate as Stakes for the 2d beft.

	1 H.
This Prize was won by Mr. *Weaver*'s Chef. M. *Small Profit*, 14 H. ———————	1

Mr.

	H.
Mr. *Tedway's* Grey M. *Merry Lass*, 13 H. 1 I.	2
Mr. *Porter's* Grey H. *Luck at last*, 14 H.	dif

On the following Day, upon this Course, a 30 *l.* Plate was run for, free only for such 5 Year Olds as never won a Plate. *wt.* 9 *st.* one Heat, 2 Guineas Entrance.

This Prize was won by	H.
The Earl of *Hallifax's* Grey H. *Grey Sore-Heels*	1
Mr. *Williams's* Bay M. *White Nose*	2
Mr. *Chetwind's* Brown H. *Forester*	3
Mr. *Humberstone's* Grey H. *Blue Ribbon*	4
Mr. *Grosvenor's* Bay H. *Locket*	5
Mr. *Thompson's* Bay G. *Merry Harrier*	6
Mr. *Rawson's* Black H. *Smiling Tom*	7
Mr. *Brewster's* Chesf. M. *Miss Ayre*	8
Mr. *Hall's* Grey H. *Now or never*	9
Sir *Robert Fagg's* Brown H. *Bully*	10
Mr. *Banks's* Black H. *Trifle-Time*	11

On the 9th *ditto*, on the same Course, a 20 *l.* Plate was run for, free only for such as never won above 10 Guineas, *wt.* 10 *st.* 2 Guineas Entrance.

This Prize was won by	H.	H.
Mr. *Deighton's* Grey M. 5 Years Old	1	1
Mr. *Banks's* Bay M. *Bonny-Buttocks*	2	dif

The last Prize of this Meeting was the Ladies Plate of 90 *l.* value, on the following Day, free only for such 6 Year Olds, as never won a King's Plate, *wt.* 9 *st.* 6 Guineas Entrance.

This

This Prize was won by	H. 1	H. 2
Mr. *Benson*'s Bay H. *Now run Johnson*	1	1
Mr. *Humberstone*'s Bay G. *Blue Scheme*	3	2
Lord *Gower*'s Bay M. *Diana*	2	3
Sir *Robert Fagg*'s Chef. M. *Fanny*	4	dif
Dutchefs of *Ancaster*'s Chef. M. *Miss Pert*	5	dr.

COVENTRY, 1731.

ON the 27th of *July*, a Purse of 50 Guineas was run for at *Coventry*, being a Present to the City from His Royal Higness the Prince of *Wales*. This Prize was free only for six Year Olds, *wt.* 12 *st.* and won by the

	1 H.	2 H.
Earl of *Hallifax*'s Bay H. *Grispin*	1	1
Mr. *Neale*'s Black H. *Sloven*	3	2
Mr. *Cornwall*'s dark Chef. H. *Prince-of-Wales*	2	dr.

On the following Day, on the same Course, was 10 Guineas for Galloways, 10 *st.* the highest give and take, and won by

	1 H.	2 H.
Mr. *Coles*'s Black G. *Little-Esquire*, 13 H. 3 I. $\frac{1}{4}$.	1	1
Mr. *Neale*'s Chef. M. *Rattle*, 13 H. 1 I. $\frac{3}{4}$	2	2
Sir *Adolph. Oughton*'s Bay M. *Smiling-Molly*, 14 H.	dis	

On the same Course, on the 29th *ditto*, a Purse of 20 Gunieas was run for, *wt.* 11 *st.* and the Winner to be sold for 50 Guineas.

	1 H.	2 H.
This Prize was won by Mr. *Neale*'s Chef. M. *Peggy-grieves-me*	1	1
Mr. *Mackworth*'s Roan H. *Now-or-never*	2	dr.

* * * * * * * * * * * * * * * * * *

EDINBURGH, 1731.

ON the 9th Day of *August*, the King's Plate was run for at *Edinburgh*; consisting of a Gold Tea-Pot of 100 Guineas Value; and being for six Year Olds, carrying 10 *st*. There started for the same the six following.

	1 H.	2 H.
M. *Thompson's* Grey M. *Miss-Brigham*, bred by Mr. *Brigham* got by *Smiling-Tom* ———	1	1
Capt. *David Cunningham's* Grey G. *Ruffler*———	3	2
Mr. *Lockart's* Grey H. *Dragoon*———	2	*dis*
Sir *James Cunningham's* Bay H. *White foot* ———	*dis*	
Sir *William Maxwell's* Bay G. *Clumsey-Cloakbag* ———	*dis*	
Mr. *Whiteford's* Grey G. *Clumsy*———	*dis*	

✥✥✥✥✥✥✥✥✥✥✥✥✥✥

BERKSHIRE, 1731.

EAST-ILSLY.

ON the 24th Day of *May*, a Purse of 10 Guin. was run for at *Ilsly*, free only for Galloways, 9 *st*. the highest give and take; to enter six Days before, paying one Guinea, or two at the Post: Which Prize was won by

	1 H.	2 H.
Sir *Hen. Inglesield's* Bay G. *Marlington*, 13 H. 3 I. ⸻	1	1
Lord *Hamilton's* Grey M. *Northern-Nancy*. 13 H. 2 I. ⸻	3	2
Mr. *Sheppard's* Bay M. *Bay-joke*, 13 H. 3 I. ¾. ⸻	2	dr.
Mr. *Thompson's* Grey M. *Black-a-Top*, 13 H. 3 I. ½, ½ qr. ⸻	dis	

On the 25th *ditto*, on the same Course, a Purse of 20 Guineas was run for, free only for such as never won 50 Guineas; *wt.* 10 *st.* to enter six Days before, paying 2 Guin. or 4 at the Post.

	1 H.
This Prize was won by	
Mr. *Sheppard's* Bay G. *Stay-till-I-come*	1
Mr. *Garrard's* Bay H. *Silver-Tail*⸻	dis
Mr. *Blunt's* Bay M. *Northern-Lass* ⸻	dis

READING.

On the 13th Day of *July*, a Purse of 30 Guineas was run for at *Reading*, free only for such as never
won

won 30 Guineas; *wt.* 10 *ft.* Entr. 2 Guin. or 4 at the Poſt.

This Prize was won by	1 H.	2 H.	3 H.	4 H.
Mr. *Vaughan*'s Black H. *Crutches*	3	1	2	1
Lord *Haverſham*'s Cheſ. M. } *Creeping Molly* ———	1	3	3	2
Mr. *Sheppard*'s Bay H. *Foreigner*	2	2	1	diſ
Mr. *South*'s Cheſ. H. *White* } *Stockings* ———	5	4	dr.	
Mr. *Orm*'s Cheſ. G. *Nicholina*——	4	5	diſ	
Mr. *Hall*'s Grey G. *Stradler* ——	diſ			
Mr. *Forteſcue*'s Grey H. *Surley*——	diſ			

On the following Day, on the ſame Courſe, a Purſe of 20 Guineas was run for, free only for ſuch as never won 20 Guineas, 14 Hands, to carry 9 *ft.* and to give or take, if higher or lower: Entr. 1 Guin. or 2 at the Poſt.

This Prize was won by	1 H.	2 H.	3 H.
Sir *Henry Inglefield*'s Bay G. *Marlington*, 13 H. 3 I.———	6	1	1
Lord *Hamilton*'s Grey M. *Northern-Nancy* 13 H. 2 I. ¼———	1	5	2
Dr. *Bonas*'s Bay H. *Squirrel*, 14 H. 1 I. ——	3	3	3
Mr. *Harvey*'s Bay H. *Whipper-Snapper*, 14 H. 1 I.———	7	2	dr.
Earl of *Albemarle*'s Brown H. *Merry-Man*, 14 H. 1 I. ———	2	4	dr.
Mr. *Kirby*'s Grey M. *Miſs-Pert*, 14 H. 1 I.———	4	dr.	
Mr. *Child*'s Dun G. *Fox*, 14 H. 1 I. ¾	5	diſ	
Mr. *Thorp*'s Cheſ. M. *Miſs-Muſcovy*, 13 H. 2 I. ¼———	8	dr.	
Mr. *Henow*'s Bay G. *Bumper*, 13 H. 2 I. ———	diſ		

2　　　　　　　　　　　　On

On the 15th *ditto*, on the fame Courfe, a Prize
of 25 Guineas Value was run for, free only for fuch
Hunters as never won 5 Guineas, *wt.* 12 *ft* Entr.
one Guin. or two at the Poft: the Winner to be
fold for 30 Guin.

This Prize was won by	1 H.	2 H.
Mr. *Boot*'s Brown G. *Ruff-Country-Dick*	1	1
Mr. *Fortefcue*'s Grey H. *Surley* ———	2	2
Mr. *Kirby*'s Grey M. *Mifs-Pert* ———	3	*dif*
Mr. *Wright*'s Sorrel G. *Helfey* ———	*dif*	
Mr. *Salisbury*'s Chef. H. *Squirrel* ———	*dif*	

A B I N G T O N.

On the 15th Day of *Sept.* a Purfe of 20 Guineas
was run for at *Abington*, free only for fuch as never
won 30 Guineas; *wt.* 11 *ft.* 2 Guineas Entr. and
won by

	1 H.	2 H.
Mr. *Hifield*'s Grey G. *Single-Pooper* ———	1	1
Mr. *Coles*'s Bay H. *White-foot* ———	2	*dr.*
A Hack to Qualify ———	*dif*	

On the following Day, on the fame Courfe, was
15 Guineas for Galloways; 9 *ft.* the higheft give
and take: one Guinea Entr. and won by

	1 H.	2 H.
Mr. *Coles*'s Black G. *Little-Efquire* ———	1	1
Mr. *Penruddock*'s Chef. M. *Mifs-Poppet* ———	2	2
Dr. *Bonas*'s Brown H. *Tom-Tit* ———	*dif*	

On the 17th *ditto*, on this Courfe, a Purfe
of 30 Guineas was run for, free only for fuch as
neves

D

never won 50 Guineas; *wt.* 12 *st.* 2 Guin. Entr. and won by

	H.
Mr. *Thatcher*'s Bay M. *Fair-Rosamond*	1
Mr. *How*'s Grey M. ——————	*dif*
A Hack to Qualify ——————	*dif*

MAIDENHEAD.

On the 27th Day of *Sept.* a Purse of 25 Guineas was run for at *Maidenhead*; *wt.* 10 *st.* 2 Guin. Entr. and won by

	1 H.	2 H.	3 H.
Mr. *Sheppard*'s Bay G. *Conqueror* ——	4	1	1
Mr. *Tuting*'s Brown M. *Cynder-Wench*	1	4	2
Mr. *Griffin*'s Grey H. *Smugler* ——	2	2	4
Mr. *Woodman*'s Grey H. *Gander* ——	3	3	3

On the following Day, on the same Course, a Purse of 10 Guineas was run for; 14 Hands to carry 9 *st.* and to give or take, if higher or lower: one Guin. Entr.

This Prize was won by

	1 H.	2 H.	3 H.
Mr. *Selby*'s Brown H. *Swallow*, 14 H. ¼ I. ——————	4	1	1
Mr. *Tuting*'s Brown M. *Cynder-Wench*, 14 H. 1 I. ——————	1	3	3
Mr. *Banks*'s Bay G. *Spavins-and-Curbs*, 13 H. 3 I. ½ ——	3	2	2
Mr. *Woodman*'s Black M. *Creeping-Kate*, 14 H. ——————	2	*dif*	

LA M-

LAMBORN.

On the 12th of *October*, a Purse of 20 Guineas was run for at *Lamborn*, free only for such as never won above 40 Guineas; *wt.* 10 *st.* and won by

	1 H.	2 H.
Mr. *Sheppard*'s Bay G. *Stay-till-I-come*	1	1
Mr. *Plampin*'s Grey G. *Single-Peeper* ——	2	2
Mr. *Thatcher*'s Bay M. *Fair-Rosamond* ——	3	3
Sir *Robert Fagg*'s Chef. H. *Coach-Horse*	4	4
Mr. *Willis*'s Grey M. *Miss-Dove* ——————	dis	
Mr. *Mansfield*'s Black G. *Tinker.* ————	dis	

On the same Course, on the 14th *ditto*, was 10 Guineas for Galloways; 9 *st.* the highest give and take, and won by

	1 H.	2 H.
Mr. *Packer*'s Bay H. *Tryal,* 13 H. 3 I.	1	1
Mr. *Sheppard*'s Bay M. *Whimsey,* 13 H. 3 I. ½ }	2	2
Mr. *Beardwell*'s Chef. M. *Diana,* 13 H. 2 I. }	dis	

'Tis reported as certain, that in the succeeding Year 1732, the best Prize at this Place will be 30 Guineas at least, for maiden Horses; and that the Galloway Plate will be 20 Guineas; and the Meeting begin on *Easter-Tuesday.*

BEDFORDSHIRE, 1731.

POTTON.

ON the 13th Day of *July*, a Purse of 50 Guineas was run for at *Potton*, and on the following Day a Plate of 20 *l.* Value; but Sir *Arthur Haſle-rige's* Cheſnut Gelding, *Poor-Robin*, ſtarted alone for the firſt, and his Bay Mare *Sweet-Maidenhead* for the ſecond of theſe Prizes: on the ſecond of which Days, upon this Courſe, a Prize of 10 Guineas Value was run for, being the Preſent of Sir *Roger Bur-gain* Bart. and being for Galloways, 9 *ſt.* the higheſt give and take: Which Prize was won by

	1 H.	2 H.
Mr. *Holland's* Grey G. ———————	1	1
Mr. *Grandy's* Dun M. *Gillian-of-Croydon*	2	2
Mr. *Johnson's* Cheſ. M. ———————	diſ	

Town of BEDFORD.

On the 24th Day of *Auguſt*, a Purſe of 30 Guin: was run for at *Bedford*, free only for ſuch as never won above 30 Guin. *wt.* 10 *ſt.* to enter on the 17th *ditto*, paying 2 Guin. Stakes for the 2d beſt.

There ſtarted for the ſame the ten following.

	1 H.	2 H.
Mr. *Coles's* Grey M. *Small-Hopes* ———————	1	1
Mr. *Heneage's* Bay H. *White-Noſe* ———————	2	2
Mr. *How's* Bay H. *King's-Fiſher* ———————	3	dr.
Mr. *Major's* Grey G. *White-Stockings* ———	4	dr.

Mr.

			1 H.
Sir *H. Monoux*'s Bay G. *Roger-de-Coverly*			dif
Mr. *Williams*'s Black H. *Sloven* ———			dif
Mr. *Harvey*'s Sorrel H. *Farmer* ———			dif
Capt. *Backwell*'s Chef. M. *Will-if-I-can*			dif
Mr. *Newton*'s Chef. M. *Mifs-Maggot* ———			dif
Mr. *Vaughan*'s Black H. *Tom-of-ten-thoufand* ———			dif

On the following Day, upon this Courfe, a Purfe of 20 Guineas was run for, free only for fuch Galloways as never won above 20 Guin. 9 *ft*. the higheft give and take: to enter on the 18th *ditto*, paying 1 Guinea.

	1 H.	2 H.
This Prize was won by		
Mr. *Rich*'s Grey H. *Harlequin*, 13 H. 2 I. $\frac{3}{4}$. ———	1	1
Mr. *Canby*'s Chef. M. *Rattle*, 13 H. 1 I.	2	2
Mr. *Clark*'s Bay M. *Stay-till-I-come*, 13 H. 3 I. $\frac{1}{4}$. ———	3	dif
Mr. *Prince*'s Chef. H. *Lady's-Delight*, 13 H. 3 I. $\frac{1}{4}$. ———	4	dr.

A 3d and laft Prize of this Meeting, was a Purfe of 50 Guineas, on the 26th *ditto*, free for any that never won above 50 Guineas, *wt*. 12 *ft*. Which Prize was won by

	1 H.	2 H.	3 H.
Mr. *How*'s Brown H. *Penfioner* ———	2	1	1
Ld *How*'s Grey H. *Jack-of-the-Green*	1	2	2

LEIGHTON-BUZARD.

On the 1ft Day of *September*, a Purfe of 20 Guin. was run for at *Leighton*, free for fuch as never won above 30 Guin. *wt*. 10 *ft*.

D 3   The

The same was won by	1 H.	2 H.
Mr. *Sheppard*'s Bay G. *Quiet*	1	1
Mr. *Henenge*'s Bay H. *White-Nose*	3	2
Mr. *Major*'s Grey G. *White-Stockings*	4	3
Mr. *Leighton*'s Chef. G. *Dragon*	5	4
Mr. *Robinson*'s Chef. M. *Miss-Flamakin*	2	dr.
Mr. *Lowndes*'s Bay G.	dif	

On the 2d *ditto*, upon this Course, a free Purse of 50 Guineas was run for, wt. 11 st. and won by the

	1 H.	2 H.
Duke of *Ancaster*'s Grey H. *Gentleman*	1	1
Mr. *Neale*'s Chef. H. *Tarran*	2	2

If one had started alone at this Place for the 20 Guineas, he muft have paid 8 Guineas; if for the 50 Guineas, 20 Guineas towards the next Year's Plates.

BUCKINGHAMSHIRE, 1731.

NEWPORT-PAGNEL.

ON the 8th Day of *September*, a 15 l. Plate was run for at *Newport*, 14 Hands, to carry 9 st. and to give or take, if higher or lower: one Guinea and a half entr. three to ftart, and the Winner to be fold for 30 Guineas.

This Prize was won by	1 H.	2 H.
Mr. *Fleetwood*'s Roan H. *Lilliput*	1.	1
Mr. *Canby*'s Chef. M. *Rattle*	2	2
Mr. *Freeman*'s Dun M.	dif	

On

On the fame Courfe, the following Day, a Purfe of 30 Guineas was run for, free only for fuch as never won 60 Guin. wt. 12 ſt. 3 Guin. entr. ſtaked for the 2d beſt.

This Prize was won by	1 H.	2 H.	3 H.
Ld Viſcount How's Grey H. Jack-of-the-Green ———	1	1	1
Sir Robert Trogmorton's Grey H. Who-can-tell ———	2	2	3
Hon. Mr. Bettit's Grey G. Foreſter ═══	3	3	2
Capt. Chapman's Grey G. Now-or-never ———	4	4	4

Enter for each of thefe Prizes refpectively 7 Days before running.

AYLSBURY.

On the 15th of September, a Purfe of 15 l. Sterl. and on the following Day a 30 l. Plate, were run for at Aylsbury; but Mr. Rich's Grey H. Harlequin ſtarted alone for the firſt, and Mr. Sheppard's Bay G. Quiet for the 2d of theſe Prizes.

GREAT-MARLOW.

On the 23d of Sept. a 20 l. free Plate was run for at Marlow; wt. 10 ſt. and won by

	1 H.	2 H.
Mr. Woodman's Grey H. Gander———	1	1
Mr. Selby's Brown H. Swallow ———	2	2
Earl of Portmore's Bay H. Spot———	diſ	

On the following Day, upon this Courfe, a free Plate of 30 l. Value was run for; wt. 12 ſt. and won by

Mr.

	1 H.	
Mr. *Tuting*'s Brown M. *Cynder-Wench*	1	
Mr. *Woodman*'s Black M.————————	2	

On the 25th *ditto*, upon this Courfe, was a 15 *l.* Plate for Galloways, 9 *ft.* the higheft give and take, and won by

	1 H.	2 H.
Sir *Henry Inglefield*'s Bay G. *Marling-ton*, 13 H. 3 I.———————————	1	1
Lord *Hamilton*'s Grey M. *Northern-Nancy*, 13 H. 2 I.—————————	2	2

For each of thefe 3 Prizes, 3 reputed Running-Horfes, &c. were, if infifted on, obliged to ftart: the Entrance-Day was the 13th *ult.* and they enter'd for each Prize *gratis.*

AMERSHAM.

On the 30th of *Septemb.* a 20 *l.* Plate was run for at *Amerfham*, *wt.* 10 *ft.* and won by

	1 H.	2 H.	3 H.
Mr. *Griffin*'s Grey M. *Smiling-Kate*——	1	1	1
Mr. *Woodman*'s Grey H. *Gander*————	2	2	2
Mr. *Glanvil*'s Chef. H. *Spot*————	3	3	3

On the following Day, upon this Courfe, a 15 Guineas Purfe was run for, 14 Hands, to carry 9 *ft.* and to give or take, if higher or lower.

	1 H.	2 H.
This Prize was won by		
Mr. *Griffin*'s Grey H. *Smugler*, 13 H. 3 I. ¼.———————————	1	1
Mr. *Fen*'s Dun M. *Country-Kate*, 13 H. 3 I.———————————	2	2

CHE-

✠✠✠✠✠✠✠✠✠✠✠✠✠✠✠✠✠✠✠✠✠✠✠

CHESHIRE, 1731.

FARN.

IN the beginning of *March*, as usual, two Prizes were run for at *Farn*; the first of 12 *l. Sterling*, *wt.* 10 *st.* exclusive of Bridle and Saddle, one Heat.

	H.
The same was won by	
Mr. *Williams*'s Black H. *Sloven*	1
Mr. *Mackworth*'s Grey H. *Favourite*	2
Mr. *Taply*'s Grey G. *Country-Farmer*	3
Sir *Rich. Grosvenor*'s Chef. M. *Cade-Filly*	4

The second of these Prizes consisted of 36 *l. Sterl.* *wt.* also 10 *st.* besides Bridle and Saddle.

	H.
This Prize was won by	
Mr. *Williams-Wynn*'s Bay H. *Spot*	1

There started against him, Sir *Richard Grosvenor*'s Chef. H. *Terror*, and Mr. *Middleton*'s Chef. H. *Infant*; both of which, by Accidents, were distanced the first Heat.

City of WEST-CHESTER.

On the 21st Day of *April*, a 10 *l.* Plate was run for at *Chester*, being for Galloways, 9 *st.* the highest give and take.

	1st H.	2d H.
Which Prize was won by		
Sir *Ralph Ashton*'s Bay M. *Creeping-Kate*, 13 H. 3 l. ¼	1	1

Mr.

	1 H.	2 H.
Mr. *Leigh*'s Bay G. *Captain*, 13 H. 3 I. ¼ ———	2	2
Mr. *Fleetwood*'s Roan H. *Squirrel*, 13 H. 1 I. ¾ ———	1	3
Mr. *Lee*'s Black G. *Black-Jack*, 13 H. 3 I. ¾ ———	4	dif
Lord *Molyneux*'s Bay M. *Long-Megg*, 13 H. 3 I. ¼ ———	dif	
Mr. *Myddleton*'s Grey M. *Sprite*, 14 H. ———	dif	

Upon this Course the fucceeding Day, a 30 *l.* Plate was run for, free only for 6 Year Olds, *wt.* 10 *st.* exclufive of Bridle and Saddle.

This Prize was won by	1 H.	2 H.
Mr. *Myddleton*'s Grey M. *Black-a-Top* ———	1	1
Sir *Richard Grofvenor*'s Chef. H. *Hollow-Back* ———	2	2
Sir *Rowland Hill*'s Chef. H. *Caft-away* ———	dif	
Mr. *Grofvenor*'s Chef. H. *Wanton* ———	dif	

On the fame Courfe, the following Day, a 30 *l.* free Plate was run for, *wt.* alfo 10 *st.* exclufive of Bridle and Saddle.

This Prize was won by	1 H.	2 H.	3 H.
Sir *Richard Grofvenor*'s Chef. H. *Terror* ———	5	1	1
Earl of *Derby*'s Chef. H. *Tickle-Pitcher* ———	1	5	2
Mr. *Mafters*'s Bay M. *Sweet-Maid* enbead ———	2	2	3
Mr. *Mackworth*'s Grey H. *Fear-not*	3	3	dr.
			Sir

	1 H.	2 H.	3 H.
Sir *William* Middleton's Chef. H. } Scipio	4	4	dr.
Sir *Rowland* Hill's Chef. H. Who- } can-tell	dif		

WALASEY.

On the 1st *Thursday* in *May*, the six following started for the Stakes at *Walasey*, confisting, as in the preceeding Year, of 280 Guineas, *wt.* (as often obferv'd) 10 *st.*

	1 H.
Duke of *Ancafter's* Grey H.	1
Duke of *Bridgewater's* Bay H.	2
Mr. *Williams's* Bay M.	3
Sir *Richard* Grofvenor's Bay H.	4
Sir *Nathaniel* Curzon's Grey H.	5
Lord *Molineux's* Bay M.	6

TRAPEWOOD.

On the 24th Day of *July*, a free Purfe of 25 Guineas was run for at *Trape-wood*, *wt.* 11 *st.* and won by

	1 H.	2 H.
Mr. *Puleston's* Chef. H. *Surly*	1	1
Mr. *Myddleton's* Chef. H. *Infant*	2	2

On the fame Courfe, the fucceeding Day, was 10 *l.* Cafh, for Galloways, 9 *st.* the highest give and take, and won by

	1 H.	2 H.
Lady *Fleetwood's* Chef. G. *Merry* } *Barnaby*	1	1

Mifs

	1 H.	2 H.
Miſs Oldfield's Grey H. ————	2	diſt
Mr. Davenport's Bay G. ————	3	diſt
Mr. Middleton's Grey M. took the reſt and ————	diſ	

KNUTSFORD.

On the 3d Day of *Auguſt*, a free Purſe of 35 Guineas was run for at *Knutsford*, wt. loſt. 3 Guineas Entrance, and won by

	1 H.	2 H.	3 H.
Mr. Puleſton's Cheſ. H. *Surly* ————	3	1	1
Sir Nathaniel Curzon's Bay H. *Traveller* ————	1	2	2
Sir Richard Groſvenor's Cheſ. H. *Terror* ————	4	4	3
Mr. Egerton's Grey H. *Kuloan* ————	2	3	4
Mr. Mackworth's Bay H. *Truſty-Roger* ————	5	dr.	

On the following Day, on the ſame Courſe, was a 10 *l.* Plate, for Galloways, 9 *ſt.* the higheſt give and take, 15 Shillings Entrance; which Prize was won by

	1 H.	2 H.
Mr. Barton's Bay M. *Moore-Poote,* 18 H. 3 I. ¾ ————	1	1
Mr. Henly's Bay H. *Pebble-Stone,* 13 H. 3 I. ½ ————	2	2
Mr. Ball's Cheſ. M. *Miſs-Speedwell,* 13 H. 3 I. ½ ————	3	dr.
Sir Thomas Fleetwood's Grey H. *Run-now-or-hunt-for-ever* ————	diſ	

Enter for both, *Thurſday* before Running.

CONGLETON.

On the 8th Day of *August*, a Purse of 10 Guineas was run for at *Congleton*, being for Galloways, 9 *st.* the highest give and take, and won by

	1 H.
Mr. *Rhodes*'s Chef. G. *Merry-Barnaby*	1
Mr. *Puleston*'s Grey M. *Filly*	dif

NAMPTWICH.

On the 30th of *August*, a free Purse of 15 Guineas was run for at *Namptwich*, *wt.* 11 *st.* one Guinea Entrance, and won by

	1 H.	2 H.	3 H.
Mr. *Mackworth*'s Bay H. *Wanton-Willy*	1	1	3
Mr. *Egerton*'s Grey H. *Vulcan*	2	3	1
Mr. *Pilkington*'s Black H. *Kiss-in-a-Corner*	3	2	2

CUMBERLAND, 1731.

PENRITH.

ON the 23d Day of *June*, a 10 *l.* Plate was run for at *Penrith*, 14 Hands, to carry 10 *st.* and to give or take if higher or lower, 15 Shillings Entr.

	1 H.	2 H.	3 H.
This Prize was won by Mr. *Newton*'s Bay M. *Smiling-Molly* 13 H. 3 I.	1	1	1
Mr. *Rawlinson*'s Brown M. *Muslin-Face*, 13 H. 2 I.	2	2	2

E

	1 H.	2 H.	3 H.
Mr. *Barker*'s Bay M. *Collier's-Fancy*, 12 H. 3 I. ————	3	3	3
Mr *Butler*'s Chef. G. *Red-Robin*, 14 H. ½ I. ————	dif		

On the 25th *ditto*, on the same Course, a Plate of 20 *l.* Value, was run for, *wt.* 10 *ft.* One Guinea and Half Entr. which Plate was won by

	1 H.	2 H.
Mr. *Bowes*'s Chef. M. *Lady-legs* ————	1	1
Mr. *Thornton*'s Grey H. *Laſt-Time-of-asking* ————	2	2

To enter for both the 21ſt *ditto*, and 3 each Day were oblig'd to ſtart.

City of CARLISLE.

On the 26th Day of *July*, a 10 *l.* Plate was run for at *Carliſle*, free only for Galloways, 10 *ft.* the higheſt give and take, and won by

	1 H.	2 H.	3 H.
Lady *Maxwell*'s Chef. M. *Will-if-ſhe-can*, 13 H. 2 I. ¼ ————	1	1	1
Mr. *Barker*'s Bay M. *Collier's-Galloway*, 12 H. 2 I. ¼ ————	2	3	2
Mr. *Carlton*'s Grey M. *Painted-Lady*, 14 H. ————	3	2	3

On the following Day, upon this Courſe, a Plate of 10 Guineas value, was run for, being a Preſent to the City from their Members of Parliament, *wt.* 10 *ſ.* Half a Guinea Entr.

This

This Prize was won by	1 H.	2 H.	3 H.
Mr. *Cooper's* Chef. G. *Red-Robin*——	1	1	1
Mr. *Hall's* Grey G. *Batchelor* ——	2	2	2
Mr. *Thompson's* Chef. G. *Red-Robin*—	3	3	dr.
Mr. *Marshal's* Bay M. *Country-Wench*	4	dr.	

On the same Course, on the 31st *ditto*, a free Plate of 25 *l.* value, was run for, *wt.* also 10 *ft.* 2 Guineas Entr. and won by

	1 H.	2 H.
Mr. *Salkield's* Bay M. *Camilla*, got by *Almanzor* —— }	1	1
Mr. *Fenwick's* Grey G. *Smock-Face* ——	3	2
Mr. *Potts's* Grey H. *Bonny-Lad* ——	2	3

D E R B Y S H I R E. 1731.

CHESTERFIELD.

ON the 21st Day of *July*, the 40 *l.* Plate for 6 Year Olds, (being the accustomed Present to the Town by the Right Hon. the Earl of *Scarsdale*) was run for at *Chesterfield*; *wt.* 10 *ft.* 2 Guin. entrance, and won by

	1 H.	2 H.	3 H.
Mr. *Mountain's* Grey H. *Fear-not*——	2	1	1
Sir *Richard Grosvenor's* Chef. H. *Hollow-Back* —— }	1	2	2
Mr. *Grosvenor's* Chef. H. *Wanton-Will* —— }	4	3	dr.
Earl of *Portmore's* Black G. *Jack-Dam* —— }	3	dif	

On the following Day, upon this Course, was 10 Guineas for Galloways; 9 *ft.* the highest give and take; and won by

Mr.

	1 H.	2 H.
Mr. *Henly*'s Bay H. *Pebble-Stone,* 13 H. 3 I. ½. ——	1	1
Mr. *Pritchard*'s Bay G. *Who-can-tell,* 13 H. ½ I. ——	3	2
Mr. *Moody*'s Bay M. *Bonny-Honey* 13 H. 2 I. ½. ——	2	dr.

On the 23d *ditto,* upon this Course, a Purse of 20 Guineas was run for: being for 5 Year Olds, *wt.* 10 *st.* 2 Miles at a Heat.

This Prize was won by	1 H.	2 H.
Lady *Chaplin*'s Brown H. *Spot* ——	1	1
Mr. *Williams*'s Chef. H. *Almanzor* ——	2	2
Sir *Nathaniel Curzon*'s Grey H. *Iron-Sides* ——	3	3

BAKEWELL.

On the 25th Day of *August,* a Purse of 15 Guin. was run for at *Bakewell; wt.* 10 *st.* to ent. on the 20th *ditto,* paying one Guin. and three to start.

This Prize was won by	1 H.	2 H.
Mr. *Langley*'s Bay M. *Charming-Nancy*	1	1
Mr. *Steer*'s Chef. G. *Little-John* ——	2	2
Mr. *Trigg*'s Chef. G. *Pleasant-Robin* ——	dis	

On the same Course, the following Day, was a Purse of 10 Guineas for Galloways, 9 *st.* the highest give and take; 1 Guin. Entr. and won by

	1 H.	2 H.
Mr. *Longden*'s Grey G. *Cripple,* 13 H. 3 I. ——	1	1
Mr. *Austin*'s Chef. M. 13 H. 3 I. ¾ ——	2	2
Mr. *Street*'s Bay M. *Hazard* ——	dis	

The 20 Guin. for 6 Year Olds at this Place were not run for.

COUNTY DURHAM, 1731.

WORSINGHAM.

ON the 2d Day of *March*, a 10 Guin. Purse for 4 Year Olds was run for at *Worsingham*; *wt.* 10 ʃt. to ent. on the 26th Day of *Febr.* paying one Pound seven Shillings and Six-pence.

	1 H.	2 H.	3 H.
This Prize was won by			
Mr. *Twizle*'s Grey H. *Country-Man*	3	1	1
Mr. *Wood*'s Bay H. *Post-Boy*	2	2	2
Mr. *Wilson*'s Bay G.	1	dis	

BISHOP-AUKLAND.

On the 11th Day of *May*, a Purse of 20 Guin. was run for at *Aukland*, free only for such 5 Year Olds as never started before, *wt.* 10 ʃt. and won by

	1 H.
Mr. *Charlton*'s Grey H. *Sprightly*	1
Mr. *Hilton*'s Bay M.	2
Lord *Darcy*'s Bay H. *Monkey*	3
Mr. *Shuttleworth*'s Bay H.	4

On the 12th *ditto*, on the same Course, a free Purse of 15 Guin. was run for; *wt.* 10 ʃt. and won by

	1 H.	2 H.	3 H.
Mr. *Hudson*'s Cheʃ. H. *Fair-Play*	1	1	2
Mr. *Stevenson*'s Cheʃ. M. *Miʃs-Stevenson*	3	2	1
Mr. *Mitchel*'s Bay G.	2	dis	

E 3   The

The 10 Guineas advertised for the following Day at this Place, were not run for.

City of DURHAM.

On the 25th Day of *May*, a 20 *l.* Plate was run for at *Durham*, free only for 5 Year Olds, *wt. 9 ft.* 3 Miles at a Heat.

This Prize was won by	1 H.	2 H.	3 H.
Mr. *Laws*'s Black G. ——————	3	1	1
Mr. *Redshaw*'s Bay G. ——————	2	3	3
Mr. *Davinson*'s Bay M. ——————	4	4	2
Mr. *Unthank*'s Chef. G. ——————	1	5	dif
Mr. *Ovington*'s Bay G. ——————	5	2	dif

On the following Day, at the same City, a Purse of 12 Guin. was run for, being for 4 Year Olds; *wt. 9 ft.* one 4 Miles Heat.

This Prize was won by	1 H.
Mr. *Richardson*'s Brown M. ——————	1
Mr. *Hornsby*'s Chef. M. ——————	2
Mr. *Woodhouse*'s Bay G. ——————	3

On the following Day, at this City, was a 10 *l.* Plate for Galloways; 9 *ft.* the highest give and take: and won by

	1 H.	2 H.	3 H.
Mr. *Newton*'s Bay M. ——————	1	1	4
Mr. *Gordon*'s Grey H. ——————	4	4	1
Mr. *Clark*'s Grey M. ——————	2	2	2
Mr. *Wright*'s Grey H. ——————	3	3	3

STOCKTON.

On the 10th Day of *July*, a 30 *l.* Plate was run for at *Stockton*, free only for 5 Year Olds, *wt.* 10 ft. and won by
Mr.

	1 H.	2 H.	3 H.
Mr. *Lister's* Grey H. *Dunkirk* ——————	1	1	5
Mr. *Wilson's* Bay H. *Carpenter* ——————	5	2	1
Mr. *Charlton's* Grey H. *Sprightly* ———	6	3	2
Mr. *Oneby's* Black G. *Batchelor* ————	3	4	4
Mr. *Henry's* M. *Constant-Stockton* ——————	4	5	3
Mr. *Binington's* Grey H. *Cast-away* ———	7	6	6
Mr. *Redshaw's* Bay G. ———————	2	7	7
Mr. *Priest's* Bay H. *Merry-P——le* ———	8	dr.	

On the following Day, upon this Course, a 12 l.
Plate was run for; 14 Hands, to carry 9 *st.* and to
give or take, if higher or lower.

	1 H.	2 H.	3 H.
This Prize was won by			
Mr. *Bathurst's* Grey H. *Dusty-Mil-ler*, 14 H. 3 I. ¾ ——————	1	1	4
Mr. *Cook's* Chef. M. *Modesty*, 13 H. 3 I. ¼ ——————	4	2	1
Mr. *Jefferson's* Grey H. 13 H. 2 I. ½	3	3	2
Mr. *Bacon's* Grey M. *Silver-Locks*, 14 H. ¾ I. ——————	2	4	3

On the 12th *ditto*, on the same Course, was a
20 l. Plate for 4 Year Olds; *wt.* 9 *st.* one Heat: and
won by

	1 H.
Mr. *Rawlings's* Chef. M. ————————	1
Mr. *Dodson's* Bay H. *Spider* —————	2
Mr. *Turner's* Bay H. *Trincalo* ————	3
Mr. *Cowling's* Chef. M. *White-Nose*———	4
Mr. *Byers's* Grey H. ———————	5
Mr. *Scafe's* Grey M. *Little-Bitch* ——	6
Mr. *Smith's* Bay G. ———————	7

CHES-

CHESTER IN THE STREET.

On the 26th of *July*, a Purse of 10 Guineas was run for at *Chester*, free only for such as were not more than 4 Lunar Months over 6 Years old, nor never won 10 Guin. *wt.* 10*ß.* one Guin. Entr.

This Prize was won by	1 H.	2 H.	3 H.
Sir *Ralph Conyers*'s Chef. M. *Dome-justice*	1	1	3
Mr. *Ingleby*'s Bay G.	4	3	1
Mr. *Byers*'s Bay M.	2	2	2
Mr. *Crow*'s Grey M.	3	dif	

On the 28th *ditto*, upon this Course, a Purse of 15 Guineas was run for, free only for such as did not exceed 4 Lunar Months over 5 Years old, nor ever won 15 Guin. wt. 9*ß.* one Guinea and a half Entr.

This Prize was won by	1 H.	2 H.	3 H.
Mr. *Newton*'s Bay M.	1	1	3
Mr. *Ingleby*'s Bay M.	3	2	1
Mr. *Ovington*'s Bay G.	2	3	2
Mr. *Jacques*'s Grey M.	4	4	4

Enter for both on the 22d *ditto*; and four each Day were obliged to start.

WINLATON.

On the 14th Day of *August*, a Plate of 13 *l.* Value, being the Gift of *Ambrose Crawley* Esq; was run for at *Winlaton*, 14 Hands, to carry 10*ß.* and to give and take, if higher or lower: to ent. on the 7th *ditto*, paying 25 *Skil.* four to start.

This

This Prize was won by	1 H.	2 H.	3 H.
Mr. *Storey*'s Chef. H. ———————	1	1	3
Mr. *Arrowsmith*'s Bay G. ———————	2	4	1
Mr. *Fenwick*'s Chef. M. ———————	3	2	2
Mr. *Hill*'s Grey G. ———————	5	3	4
Mr. *Harrison*'s Chef. M. ———————	4	dif	

HETGHINGTON

On the 24th Day of *August*, a Purfe of 20 Guin. was run for at *Heighington*, free only for fuch as were not five Years old till the firft Day of *January* laft; *wt. 9 ft.* 2 Guin. Entr.

Which Prize was won by	1 H.	2 H.
Mr. *Elßob*'s Bay H. *Monkey* ———————	1	1
Mr. *Fish*'s Bay H. *Surly* ———————	3	2
Mr. *Bateman*'s Bay H. *Fortunatus* ———	2	3

On the following Day, on the fame Courfe, was 10 Guineas for Galloways: 9 ft. the higheft give or take: one Guin. Entr. there ftarted for the fame the three following.

	1 H.	2 H.	3 H.
Mr. *Newton*'s Chef. M. ———————	2	3	1
Mr. *Bink*'s Bay M. ———————	3	2	2
Mr. *Nesham*'s Bay H. ———————	1	1	dif

Thefe three are figur'd as they came in; but in the 2d Heat the Chef. Mare was charged with foul Play, and thereupon declared difqualified to ftart again: however, fhe would and did ftart, but the Prize was given to the Bay Mare. But 'tis thought the fame will create a Conteft at Law.

On the following Day, upon this Courfe, a Purfe of 15 Guin. was run for, free only for fuch as were
not

not four Years old till the 1st Day of the preceding *June*; *wt*. 9 *ft*. one Heat: 1 Guin. ½ Entr. Which Prize was won by

	H.
Mr. *Cowlins*'s Chef. M. *White-Nose* ———	1
Hon. Mr. *Vane*'s Bay M. ———————	2
Mr. *Akenfide*'s Chef. G. *Wasp* ———	3
Mr. *Forfter*'s Grey H. *Surly* ———	4

On the 27th *ditto*, upon this Courfe, a Purfe of 20 Guineas was run for, free only for fuch as were not fix Years old till the 1st Day of the preceding *January*; *wt*. 10 *ft*. 2 Guin. Ent.

This Prize was won by	1 H.	2 H.
Mr. *Salkeild*'s Bay M. *Camila* ———	1	1
Mr. *Bowes*'s Grey M. *Lady-Legs* ———	3	2
Mr. *Winfhip*'s Bay M. *Favourite* ———	2	3

Enter for all four on the 18th *ditto*.

BERNARD-CASTLE.

On the 31ft Day of *Auguft*, a Purfe of 25 Guin. (being a Prefent to the Town by the Hon. *Hen. Vane* Efq;) was run for at *Bernard-Caftle*, free only for fix Year Olds; *wt*. 10 *ft*. 2 Guin. Entr.

This Prize was won by	1 H.	2 H.
Mr. *Jennifon*'s Bay M. *Maidenhead* ———	1	1
Mr. *Bowes*'s Black H. *Othello* ———	2	2

On the 1ft of *Septemb*. upon this Courfe, a Purfe of 20 Guin. was run for; 14 Hands, to carry 10 *ft*. and to give or take, if higher or lower: one Guin. Entr.

This

	1 H.	2 H.	3 H.
This Prize was won by			
Mr. *Scot*'s Bay H. *Tryal*, 13 H. 2 I. ½	1	1	1
Mr. *Hartford*'s Grey H. *Spot*, 13 H. 3 I.	2	2	dif

On the 2d *ditto*, on the same Course, a Purse of 25 Guin. (being the Present of *George Bowes* Esq; Member of Parliament for this County of *Durham*) free only for such as were not then more than six Lunar Months over five Years old; *wt.* 10 ß. 2 Miles at a Heat, 2 Guin. Entr.

	1 H.	2 H.	3 H.
This Prize was won by			
Mr. *Bathurst*'s Chef. H. *Dainty-Davy*	1	1	2
Mr. *March*'s Chef. H. *Surly*	3	4	1
Mr. *Smales*'s Bay H. *Smales-Chiders*	2	3	3
Mr. *Jackson*'s Grey H. *Better-Luck*	5	2	4
Mr. *Vary*'s Chef. G. *Farmer*	4	dif	
Mr. *Cathorn*'s Chef. M. *Luckless*	dif		
Mr. *Mitchel*'s Bay G.	dif		

On the 3d *ditto*, on the same Course, a free Plate, consisting of a Gold Cup of 50 Guineas Value, was run for; *wt.* 10 ß. 3 Guin. Entr. and won by

	1 H.	2 H.	3 H.
Mr. *Brewster*'s Bay M. *Miss-Nesham*	1	1	3
Mr. *Bright*'s Brown M. *Emma*	4	3	1
Mr. *Barton*'s Bay M. *Favourite*	2	4	2
Mr. *Hodgson*'s Chef. H. *Fair-play*	5	2	4
Mr. *Smith*'s Grey H. *Midge*	3	dif	
Sir *Ralph Milbank*'s Grey H. *Dufty-Miller*	dif		
Mr. *Bowes*'s Chef. M. *Lady-Legs*	dif		

Enter for all four of these Prizes on the 28th of *August*; and four, if insisted on, were obliged each Day to start.

SUNDERLAND.

On the 15th Day of Septemb. a Plate of 25 l. Value was run for at *Sunderland*, free only for such Four Year Olds as never won a Plate; wt. 9 st. 4 Miles at a Heat, 2 Guin. Entr.

Which Prize was won by	1H.	2H.	3H.
Mr. *Lampton's* Dun H. *Sprightly*	4	1	1
Mr. *Elstob's* Bay M. *Shadow*	1	2	2
Mr. *Croft's* Grey H.	5	3	4
Mr. *Wilde's* Bay M.	6	6	3
Sir *John Stapylton's* Grey M. *Sweet-if-you-love-me-come-away*	2	4	dis
Mr. *Charlton's* Chef. H. *Conjurer*	3	5	dr.

On the 16th *ditto*, on the same Course, a 2d 25 l. Plate was run for, 14 Hands, to carry 10 st. and to give or take, if higher or lower: 2 Guin. Entr.

This Prize was won by	1H.	2H.	3H.
Mr. *Lampton's* Grey H. *Bonny-Batchelor*, 14 H.	1	1	1
Mr. *Armstrong's* Bay M. *Jenny-the-Baker*, 13 H. 2 I. ½	2	2	2

On the 17th Day of this Month, a Gold Cup of 40 l. Value was run for on the same Course, free only for such five Year Olds as never won a Plate of above 20 Guineas Value; wt. 10 st. 3 Guin. Entr.

Which Prize was won by	1H.	2H.	3H.	4H.
Mr. *Routh's* Chef. M. *Barberry*	3	1	4	1
Mr. *Thompson's* Bay H. *No-Trust-like-Tryal*	6	4	1	2
Mr. *Twizle's* White H. *Sober-Cuddy*	1	6	5	3

Mr.

	1 H.	2 H.	3 H.
Mr. *Dowthwait*'s Sorrel M. *Smiling-Molly* ———	4	2	2
Mr. *Redshaw*'s Bay G. *Wax-Work* ———	2	5	3
Mr. *Charlton*'s Grey H. *Sprightly*	5	4	6

On the following Day, upon the same Course, a 20 *l*. Plate was run for, *wt*. 10 *st*. and won by

	1 H.	2 H.	3 H.
Sir *John Swinburn*'s Grey M. *Sweet-Lips* ———	1	1	3
Mr. *Hope*'s Grey G. *Patch*———	3	2	1
Mr. *Beacon*'s Grey M. *Smiling-Betty*—	2	3	2

DORSETSHIRE, 1731.

BLANDFORD.

ON the 16th Day of *June*, a Purse of 10 Guin. was run for at *Blandford*, free only for Galloways, 9 *st*. the highest give and take: to ent. 7 Days before, paying half a Guin. or double at the Post.

	1 H.	2 H.
This Prize was won by Mr. *Penruddock*'s Chef. M. *Miss-Poppet*	1	
Mr. *Trye*'s Bay M.———	*dis*	

On the following Day, on this Course, a Purse of 20 Guineas was run for, free only for such as were used as Hunters in the past Season; *wt*. 12 *st*. to ent. 7 Days before, paying 2 Guineas or 5 at the Post.

F   The

	1 H.	2 H.	3 H.
The same was won by			
Mr. *Long*'s Bay G. *Caſt-away*	1	2	1
Mr. *Fownes*'s Cheſ. H.	2	1	2
Mr. *Trye*'s Bay M.	diſ		
Mr. ——— Bay M.	diſ		

The 30 Guineas advertiſed for the 16th *ult.* at this Place, were not run for.

ESSEX, 1731.

EPPING.

ON the 18th Day of *May*, the following four ſtarted for a 15 *l.* Place at *Epping*; the higheſt Horſe to carry 11 *ſt.* and to allow Abatement proportionable to all other.

	1 H.	2 H.
Mr. *Clark*'s Grey M. *Miſs-Mag-got*, 14 H. 1 I.	1	1
Mr. *Chapman*'s Cheſ. G. *Spot*, 13 H. 2 I.	2	2
Mr. *Wans*'s Cheſ. M. 13 H. ½ I.	diſ	
Mr. *Berrisfield*'s Bay G.	diſ	

On the 20th *ditto*, upon this Courſe, was 10 Guin. for Galloways, 9 *ſt.* the higheſt give and take, and won by

	1 H.	2 H.
Mr. *Wans*'s Cheſ. M. 13 H. ½ I.	1	1
Mr. *Flanders*'s Bay M. *Miſs-Prue*, 13 H. 2 I.	2	2

Mr.

	1 H.	2 H.
Mr. *Chapman*'s Chef. G. *Spot*, 13 H. 2 I.	3	3
Mr. *Farmer*'s Bay M. 13 H. 3 I.———	dif	
Mr. *Ball*'s G. *Favourite*———————	dif	

On the 3d of *Novemb.* on the fame Courfe, a 15 *l.* Plate was run for, 14 Hands, to carry 9 *ſt.* and to give or take, if higher or lower.

	1 H.	2 H.	3 H.
This Prize was won by Mr. *Griffin*'s Grey M. *Country-Kate,* 14 H. 1 I. ¼.———————	3	1	1
Mr. *Banks*'s Bay G. *Squirrel*, 14 H. ¼ I.——— — — — — —	1	2	2
Mr. *Bertie*'s Black H. *Cripple*, 13 H. 3 I.———————	2	dif	

On the 4th *ditto,* on the fame Courfe, a 10 *l.* Plate was run for, 14 Hands, to carry 10 *ſt.* and to give or take, if higher or lower.

	1 H.	2 H.
Which Prize was won by Mr. *Elwood*'s Chef. H. *Smiling-Ball*, 14 H. 1 I.———————	1	1
Mr. *Smith*'s Grey G. *Stay-till-I-come*, 14 H. ¼ I.———————	2	2
Mr. *Flanders*'s Bay M. *Miſs-Prue,* 13 H. 2 I. ¼.———————	3	3

GLOU-

GLOUCESTERSHIRE, 1731.

TEWKSBURY.

ON the 23d Day of *September*, a 30 *l.* free Purse was run for at *Tewksbury*, wt. 11 *st.* to enter the *Saturday* before, paying 2 Guineas.

	1 H.	2 H.
This Prize was won by		
Mr. *Kirby*'s Bay M. *Statira* ————	1	1
Mr. *Neal*'s Chef. H. *Dragon* ————	2	2

On the same Course, on the following Day, was 12 Guineas for Galloways, 9 *st.* the highest give and take, to enter the *Monday* before, paying one Guinea and a half.

	1 H.	2 H.
This Prize was won by		
Mr. *Kirby*'s Bay G. *Wanton-Willy*, 13 H. 3 I. ½ ————	1	1
Mr. *Canby*'s Chef. M. *Creeping-Molly*, 13 H. ¼ I. ————	2	2
Mr. *Davis*'s Chef. M. *Peggy-grieves-me*, 13 H. ½ I.	3	3

HEREFORDSHIRE, 1731.

City of HEREFORD.

ON the 16th Day of *August*, a Purse of 20 Guineas, and the usual Honorary Whip, given by

Velters

Velters Cornewall, Efq; were run for at *Hereford*, free only for fuch 4 Year Olds, as were foal'd in this County of *Hereford*, or within 5 Miles of the fame, carrying 9 *ft.* one Heat; which Heat was won by

	1 H.
Mr. *Howard*'s Grey M. ———	1
Mr. *Cornewall*'s Bay H. *Creeper*———	2
Mr. *Price*'s Chef. M. ———	3

On the 17th *ditto*, upon this Courfe, a free Purfe of 40 Guineas was run for, *wt.* 10 *ft.* and won by .

	1 H.
Mr. *Neale*'s Chef. M. *Peggy-grieves-me* ———	1
Mr. *Kirby*'s Bay M. *Statira* ———	2

On the 18th *ditto*, on the fame Courfe, was 20 *l.* for Galloways, 9 *ft.* the higheft give and take, and won by

	1 H.	2 H.	3 H.
Mr. *Hurft*'s Bay G. *Squirrel*, 13 H. 3 I. ½ ———	1	1	1
Mr. *Pritchard*'s Bay G. *Now-or-never*, 13 H. 1 I. ———	2	2	2

On the 20th *ditto*, on the fame Courfe, a Purfe of 30 *l.* Sterling, was run for, *wt.* 9 *ft.* and won by

	1 H.	2 H.	3 H.
Mr. *Cornewall*'s Chef. H. *Poft-Boy*———	2	1	1
Mr. *Goodyer*'s Grey G. ———	1	2	2
Mr. *Foley*'s Chef. M. ———	3	3	dr.

HUN-

HUNTINGDONSHIRE, 1731.

Town of HUNTINGDON.

ON the 27th Day of *July*, a free Purse of 25 *l.* Sterling, was run for at *Huntingdon*, *wt.* 10 *st.* 2 Guineas Entr. which Prize was won by

	1 H.	2 H.
Lord Viscount *How's* Grey H. *Jack-of-the-Green* ———————	1	1
Mr. *Heneage's* Bay H. *White-Nose* ———	2	2
Mr. *Fleetwood's* Brown H. *Merry-Batchelor-* ———————	3	3
Sir *Roger Burgain's* Chef. G. *Poor-Robin*	4	4
Mr. *Grifewood's* Grey G. ————————	dif	
Mr. *Hals's* Bay G. *Quidnunc* ———————	dif	

On the following Day, upon this Course, a Purse of 20 Guineas was run for, free only for Galloways, 9 *st.* the highest give and take, one Guinea and an Half Entr.

This Prize was won by	1 H.	2 H.
Mr. *Fleetwood's* Roan H. *Lilliput* ————	1	1
Mr. *Porter's* Chef. M. *Red-Joke* ———	2	2
Mr. *Grandy's* Bay G. *Squirrel* ————	3	dr

On the following Day, on the same Course, a Purse of 40 *l.* Sterling, was run for, *wt.* 11 *st.* 2 Guineas and a Half Entr. which Prize was also won by

Lord

	1 H.	2 H.
Lord *How's Jack-of-the-Green*———	1	1
Duke of *Ancaster's* Grey H. *Gentleman*	3	2
Sir *Roger Burgain's* Chef. G. *Poer-Robin*	2	3
Earl of *Portmore's* Grey H. *Spot* ———	4	dr.
Mr. *Grifewood's* Brown H. *Cripple* ———	dif	

ST. IVES.

On the 10th Day of *August*, a 10 *l*. Plate was run for at *St. Ives*, free only for Galloways, 9 *ft*. the highest give and take, and won by

	1 H.	2 H.
Mr. *Fleetwood's* Roan H. *Lilliput*———	1	1
Mr. *Holland's* Grey G.———————	2	2
Mr. *Gatwood's* Chef. H. *Touch-me-softly*	3	3

The 15 *l*. Plate at this Place, on the following Day, was given to Mr. *Fleetwood's Lilliput*, without ftarting.

A 3d and laft Prize of this Meeting, was a 20 *l*. Plate, on the 12th *ditto*, *wt*. 11 *ft*. and won by

	1 H.
Lord Vifcount *How's* Grey H. *Jack-of-the-Green*———————	1
Capt. *Chapman's* Chef. G. *Cripple*———	2
Mr. *Simpfon's* Grey G. *Bucephalus*.———	3
Mr. *Dodd's* Chef. M. *Nanny-the-fafteft*———	4

SAWTRY.

On the 2d of *September*, a 20 *l*. Plate was run for at *Sawtry*, *wt*. 9 *ft*. and the Winner to be fold for 20 Guineas,

This

	1 H.	2 H.	3 H.
This Prize was won by			
Sir *Roger Burgain*'s Bay G. *Red-cap* ──	2	1	1
Duke of *Ancaster*'s Chef. H. *Pert* ──	4	2	2
Mr. *Dawson*'s White H. *Cinnamon* ──	3	4	
Mr. *Ward*'s Chef. G. *Laft-Time-of-asking* ──	1	dif	
Mr. *Newton*'s Grey M. *Mifs Maggot* ──	dif		
Mr. *Williamfon*'s Chef. G. *Crop* ──	dif		

On the 3d *ditto*, on this Courfe, was a 10 *l.* Plate, for Galloways, 9 *ft.* the higheft give and take, and won by

	1 H.	2 H.	3 H.
Mr. *Dyer*'s Bay H. *Tack-about*, 14 H.	4	1	1
Mr. *Hals*'s Chef. G. *Stiff-Dick*, 13 H. 1 I. ──	2	2	2
Mr. *Parfons*'s Roan G. *White-Stockings*, 13 H. 2 I. $\frac{1}{4}$ ──	1	dif	
Mr. *Cumberland*'s Grey H. *Merry-Batchelor*, 13 H. 3 I. $\frac{1}{4}$ ──	3	dif	

HAMPSHIRE, 1731.

PORTSMOUTH.

ON the 13th of *Auguft*, a 10 *l.* Plate was run for at *Portfmouth*, 14 Hands, to carry 9 *ft.* and to give or take, if higher or lower; which Prize was won by

	1 H.	2 H.
Mr. *Clare*'s Grey G. *Bonny-George*, 13 H. 3 I. $\frac{1}{4}$ ──	1	1
Mr. *Knight*'s Grey H. *Cuddy*, 13 H. 3 I. $\frac{3}{4}$ ──	3	2
Mr. *Barlow*'s Bay M. *Smiling-Jenny*, 13 H. 1 I. $\frac{1}{2}$ ──	2	3

Mr.

	1 H.	2 H.
Mr. *Henley*'s Brown G. *Slugg*, 14 H. 2 I. ½	dif	
Mr. *Bridges*'s Bay G. *Tickle-me-quickly*, 14 H. 3 I. ¼	dif	
Mr. *Calamore*'s Brown H. *Crippl'd-Tony*, 14 H. 3 I. ½	dif	

PETERSFIELD.

On the 25th *ditto*, a Purse of 10 Guineas, was run for at *Petersfield*, 14 Hands, to carry 10 ſt. and to give or take, if higher or lower.

	1 H.	2 H.
This Prize was won by Mr. *Andrews*'s Grey H. *Flippant*, 14 H.	1	1
Mr. *Polling*'s Bay G. *Dull Bull*, 14 H. 1 I.	2	2
Mr. *Heberden*'s Grey M. *Smiling-Molly*, 13 H. 2 I.	dif	
Mr. *Bradley*'s Brown M. *Sloven*, 14 H. 2 I.	dif	
Mr. *Pescod*'s Grey M. *Will-if-I-can*, 12 H. 2 I.	dif	
Mr. *Eames*'s Black G. *Lowſter*.	dif	

RINGWOOD.

On the 2d of *September*, a Purſe of 10 Guineas, was run for at *Ringwood*, wt. 10 ſt. and won by

	1 H.	2 H.	3 H.
Mr. *Willis*'s Grey M. *Miſs-Dove*, got by *Windham*	1	1	3
Earl of *Shaftesbury*'s Bay H. *Ruby*	3	2	1
Mr. *Mansfield*'s Black G. *Tinker*	2	3	2
Mr. *Carvill*'s Bay H.	5	dif	
Mr. *Hinkman*'s Grey M. *Slugg*	4	dr.	
Mr. *Wake*'s Dun M. *Mule*	6	dr.	
Mr. *Lucas*'s Black M.	dif		

HERT-

HERTFORDSHIRE, 1731.

BARNET.

ON the 10th Day of *July*, at *Barnet*, Mr. *Hales's* Grey Mare beat Mr. *Eachard's* Bay Mare; 8 *ſt.* the loweſt give or take, 2 Miles, 20 Guin.

On the 31ſt of *Auguſt*, on the ſame Courſe, a 20 *l.* Purſe was run for, free for any that never won 30 *l.* 15 Hands, to carry 11 *ſt.* and to give or take, if higher or lower.

	1 H.	2 H.	3 H.
Which Prize was won by Sir *Robert Fagg's* Grey H. *Roſamond*, 13 H. 3 I. ¼	2	1	1
Mr. *Griffin's* Grey M. *Country-Kate*, 14 H. 1 I. ¼	1	2	2
Mr. *Grandy's* Bay G. *Squirrel*, 14 H. ½	3	3	diſ

On the 2d of *Septemb.* upon this Courſe, a Purſe of 10 Guin. was run for, free only for ſuch Galloways as never won 20 *l.* 9 *ſt.* the higheſt give and take; and won by

	1 H.	2 H.
Ld *Hamilton's* Grey M. *Northern-Nancy*, 13 H. 2 I. ¼	1	1
Mr. *Dower's* Cheſ. G. *Tom-Tit*, 13 H. 3 I. ¼	3	2
Mr. *Bonas's* Bay H. *Black-Legs*, 14 H.	2	3
Mr. *Tate's* Dun M. *Smiling-Molly*, 13 H. 2 I.	diſ	
Mr. *Edmund's* Bay M. *Peggy-grieves-me*, 14 H.	diſ	

On

On the 20th *ditto*, on the same Course, Mr. *Aden's* Bay H. *Squirrel*, beat Mr. *Busby's* Grey G. 3 several Heats, 9 *st.* 4 Miles a Heat: 10 *l.* also each Heat.

ODSEY.

On the 16th Day of *Sept.* a Purse of 50 Guin. was run for at *Odsey*; *wt.* 12 *st.* and won by

	1 H.	2 H.
Mr. *Robinson's* Chef. M. *Lucy-Lockit*	1	1
Earl of *Portmore's* Chef. H. *Now-or-never*	3	2
Mr. *Freeman's* Bay G. *Surly*	2	3
Mr. *Goulston's* Grey H. *Thistle-Whipper*	4	4
Duke of *Bedford's* Chef. G. *Wadey*	dif	

On the same Course, the following Day, was 15 Guineas for Galloways; 9 *st.* the highest give and take, and won by

Mr. *Goulston's* Chef. G. *Wensel*, beating Mr. *Symon's* Chef. M. *Tear-Stocking*, and Mr. *Baker's* Bay G. *Pig*.

On the same Course, the following Day, was 15 Guineas for Hunters; *wt.* 14 *st.* and won by

	1 H.	2 H.
Mr. *Erret's* Black H. *Tom-of-ten-thousand*	1	1
Mr. *Tuting's* Bay G.	2	2
Mr. *Grisewood's* Brown H. *Foxhunter*	3	3

KENT,

KENT, 1731.

BROMLEY.

Towards the latter End of the Season, a 25 *l.* Plate was run for at *Bromley*, 14 Hands, to carry 10 *ſt.* and to give or take, if higher or lower.

Which Prize was won by	1 H.	2 H.
Sir *Robert Fagg's* Grey H. *Roſamond*, 13 H. 3 I. $\frac{1}{2}$	1	1
Mr. *Banks's* Bay G. *Spavins-and-Curbs*, 14 H. $\frac{1}{4}$ I.	3	2
Mr. *Griffin's* Grey H. *Smugler*, 13 H. 3 I. $\frac{3}{4}$	2	3

On the ſame Courſe, on the following Day, a 15 *l.* Plate was run for, 14 Hands, to carry 9 *ſt.* and to give or take, if higher or lower.

Which Prize was won by	1 H.	2 H.	3 H.
Lord *Hamilton's* Grey M. *Northern-Nancy*, 13 H. 2 I.	2	1	1
Mr. *Blackland's* Grey M. *Farmers-Pleaſure*, 13 H. 2 I.	1	3	3
Mr. *Woodman's* Black M. *Creeping-Kate*, 14 H.	3	4	2
Lord *Ruſſel's* Roan G.	4	2	4

A 3d Prize of this Meeting, was a Plate of 10 *l.* Value, *wt.* 10 *ſt.* and won by

I

Mr.

	1 H.	2 H.
Mr. *Woodman*'s Black M. *Creeping-Kate*	1	1
Sir *Robert Fagg*'s Chef. G.—————	3	2
Capt. *Hasleby*'s Grey H. *Grey-Harry*——	4	3
Mr. *Smith*'s Bay G.—————	2	dr.

LANCASHIRE, 1731.

WIGAN.

ON the 7th Day of *June*, a Purse of 20 Guin. was run for at *Wigan*, free only for such as never won 40 Guineas; *wt.* 10 *s*. 1 Guin. Entr.

	1 H.	2 H.	3 H.
The same was won by			
Mr. *Mackworth*'s Grey H. *Fear-not*—	1	2	1
Mr. *Jennison*'s Ch. M. *Lancashire-Lady*	2	1	2

On the following Day, upon this Course, a 10 Guineas Purse was run for, free for Galloways; 9 *s*. the highest give and take, 1 Guin. Entr. and won by

	1 H.	2 H.
Mr. *Bracken*'s Brown G. *Rumpless*, 13 H. 1 I.—————	1	1
Mr. *Leigh*'s Black H. *Ruffler*, 14 H.——	2	2
Sir *Ralph Ashton*'s Bay M. *Creeping-Kate*, 13 H. 3 I. ½ —————	dis	

The last Prize of this Meeting, was a free Purse of 40 Guin. *wt.* 10 *s*. 2 Guin. Entr. and won by the

G   Earl

	1 H.	2 H.
Earl of *Derby*'s Chef. H. *Tickle-Pitcher*	1	1
Mr. *Jennison*'s Bay M. *Fauftina*	2	2
A Hack to *Qualify*	dif	

Enter for all three, 7 Days before ftarting for the firft of thefe Prizes: Stakes each Day for the 2d beft; and three, if infifted on, were each Day oblig'd to ftart.

CLITHERO.

Upon this Courfe, on the 24th of *June*, the following four ftarted for a Purfe of 10 Guineas, 14 Hands, to carry 9 *ft.* and to give or take, if higher or lower.

	1 H.	2 H.	3 H.
Mr. *Sidebottom*'s Chef. M. *Lady-Legs*	4	1	1
Mr. *Bracken*'s Brown G. *Young-Harlequin*	1	2	2
Mr. *Noel*'s Chef. M. *Sally-Salisbury*	2	3	3
Mr. *Lifter*'s Grey M.	3	4	4

ORMSKIRK.

On the 29th Day of *June*, a Prize of 10 *l.* Value, given by the Right Hon. the Earl of *Derby*, was run for at *Ormskirk*, free only for Galloways, 9 *ft.* the higheft give and take; and won by

	1 H.	2 H.
Mr. *Sidebottom*'s Chef. M. *Lady-Legs*	1	1
Mr. *Bracken*'s Bay G. *Bold-Harlequin*	2	2
Mr. *Watkinfon*'s Bay M. *Speckled-Foot*	3	3
Mr. *Barry*'s Black G. *Mufty*	4	4
Earl of *Derby*'s Grey G. *White-Joke*	5	dr.
Mr. *Stockley*'s Bay G. *Pudding*	dif	
Mr. *Shaw*'s Chef. H. *White-Stockings*	dif	

The

The 25 Guin. for the following Day at this Place, were not run for.

PRESTON.

On the 20th Day of *July*, a free Purse of 40 Guin. was run for at *Preston*; *wt.* 10*st.* Ent. 2 Guin. 3 to start.

	H.
There started for this Prize the three following.	
Mr. *Myddleton*'s Chef. H. *Infant*————	1
Mr. *Smith*'s Grey H. *Midge* —————	2
Mr. *Frankland*'s Chef. M. *Sweetest-when-naked* ———— }	dif

In running for this Prize, in the 1st Heat *Midge* at the two-miles Post, run on the wrong Side of the same; and tho' he immediately turn'd, yet the Accident lost him so much Ground, that 'twas positively affirmed by many, that he was beat above a Distance: But the Person intrusted with the Distance-Flag, forbearing to regard the striking of the Ending-Flag, continued to support the s^d Distance-Flag for a time after the other was drop'd; in favour of which, *Midge* had opportunity of passing the said Distance-Flag, before it was fallen. Upon which a Contest ensued; the one urging that he had won the Prize, he being capable of proving by numerous Witnesses, that *Midge* (altho' the Flag was not struck in due and proper time) was in fact distanc'd, and on that Supposition refus'd to start again: In opposition to which, Mr. *Smith* urged that the Flag was indisputably the Rule, whether conducted justly or otherwise, and that as he was not distanc'd by the s^d Flag, he insisted that he was qualify'd to start again: agreeable to which, he started, and run a 2d and 3d Heat alone, in order to dispute his Claim.

G 2

The

The Articles, however, refer Difputes to the Founders, the Majority of whom gave their Opinion in favour of *Infant*; but Mr. *Smith* refus'd to relinquifh his Claim, declaring that he would appeal to the Judgment of *Newmarket*.

On the fame Courfe, on the following Day, was 20 Guin. for Galloways; 9*ft.* the higheft give or take, 1 Guin. Entr.

This Prize was won by	1 H.	2 H.	3 H.
Mr. *Hartford*'s Grey H. *Spot*, 13 H. 3 I. $\frac{1}{2}$.	4	1	1
Mr. *Thornton*'s Grey G. *Run-now-or-hunt-for-ever*, 14 H.	1	2	2
Mr. *Bracken*'s Bay H. *Bold-Harlequin*, 13 H. 1 I.	2	3	*dif*
Sir *Ralph Afhton*'s Bay M. *Creeping-Kate*, 13 H. 3 I.	3	*dif*	
Mr. *Barton*'s Bay M. *Moore-Poote*, 13 H. 3 I. $\frac{3}{4}$. was thrown down, a Man running in her way, and thereby	*dif*		

On the 22d *ditto*, upon this Courfe, the Ladies Plate of 30 *l.* Value was run for, free only for 6 Year Olds; *wt.* 10*ft.* one Guin. and half Entr.

This Prize was won by	1 H.	2 H.
Mr. *Myddleton*'s Grey M. *Black-a-Top*	1	1
Mr. *Rawlinfon*'s Chef. H. *Whittington*	2	2

Enter for each of thefe Prizes 3 Days before running; and the Stakes each Day went to the fecond beft.

Upon this Courfe, on the 23d Day of this Month of *July*, Mr. *Myddleton*'s Grey M. *Sprite*, 9*ft.* beat Mr. *Ireland*'s Bay M. 10*ft.* 4*m.* 20 Guin.

NEW.

NEWTON.

On the 5th Day of *August*, a Purse of 10 Guin. was run for at *Newton*, free for Galloways; 9 *st.* the highest give and take; and won by

	1 H.	2 H.
Mr. *Sidebottom*'s Chef. M. *Lady-Legs* ———	1	1
Mr. *Langly*'s Bay M. ———————	2	2
Mr. *Stockly*'s Bay G. *Pudding* —————	3	3

PRESCOT.

On the 12th Day of *August*, a Purse of 10 Guin. was run for at *Prescot*, being for Galloways, 9 *st.* the highest give and take; and won by

	1 H.	2 H.
Mr. *Ball*'s Chef. M. *Miss-Speedwell* ———	2	1
Mr. *Stockley*'s Bay G. *Pudding* ——— ——	1	dis
Mr. *Shaw*'s Chef. H. *White-Stockings* ———	dis	

On the following Day, on the same Course, was 15 Guin. for Galloways; 9 *st.* the highest give and take: and won by

	1 H.	2 H.
Mr. *Sidebottom*'s Chef. M. *Lady-Legs* ———	1	1
Mr. *Langly*'s Bay M. ———————	2	2
A Hack to Qualify ———————	dis	

Town of LANCASTER.

On the 17th Day of *August*, a Prize of 20 Guin. Value was run for at *Lancaster*; 14 Hands, to carry 10 *st.* and to give or take, if higher or lower: to ent. on the 14th *ult.* paying 1 Guin. Stakes for the 2d best.

G 3

This

This Prize was won by	1 H.	2 H.
Mr. *Barton*'s Bay M. *Moore-Poote*, 14 H. ½ I.	1	1
Mr. *Bracken*'s Bay G. *Rumpless*, 13 H. 1 I.	2	2

On the following Day, on the same Course, was a 10 *l.* Plate for Galloways; 10 *st.* the highest give and take: to ent. the same Day, paying half a Guin. Stakes also for the 2d best.

This Prize was won by	1 H.	2 H.
Mr. *Ball*'s Chef. M. *Miss-Speedwell*, 13 H. 3 I.	1	1
Mr. *Nelson*'s Chef. H. —— ——	2	2
Mr. ———— Chef. Galloway ——		
Mr. *Tennant*'s Black M. she broke a Leg in running the 2d Heat ——		

The 50 *l.* Plate advertised for the following Day at this Place, was not then run for.

On the 15th Day of *Septemb.* upon this Course, a Purse of 20 Guin. was run for, free only for Galloways; 9 *st.* the highest give and take: 1 Guin. Entr.

Which Prize was won by	1 H.	2 H.	3 H.
Mr. *Bracken*'s Bay G. *Rumpless*, 13 H. 1 I.	2	1	1
Mr. *Fish*'s Bay H. ————	1	3	3
Mr. *Ball*'s Bay M. *Miss-Speedwell*, 13 H. 3 I.	3	2	2

On the 16th *ditto*, on the same Course, a 50 *l.* Plate was run for, being free, and the *wt.* 11 *st.*

The same was won by	1 H.	2 H.	3 H.
Mr. *Thornton*'s Bay H. *Dumplin* ——	5	1	1
Mr. *Barton*'s Bay M. *Moore-Poote* ——	1	4	3

Mr.

	1 H.	2 H.	3 H.
Mr. *Thornton*'s Grey G. *Creeper* ———	2	2	4
Mr. *Salkield*'s Bay M. *Camilla* ———	3	3	2
Mr. *Vavasor*'s Black H. *Black-Tom* ———	4	5	5

On the following Day, the Stakes or Entrance-Money for this 50 *l*. Plate, confisting of 17 Guin. was run for by Hunters; *wt.* 11 *ft.* and won by

	H.	H.
Mr. *Machel*'s Bay M. ———	3.	1
Mr. *Bennyson*'s Grey M. ———	1	*dif*
Mr. *Bradborn*'s Bay G. ———	2	*dif*

On the 18th *ditto*, upon this Courfe, was 10 Guineas for Galloways; 9 *ft.* the highest give and take: and won by

	1 H.	2 H.
Mr. *Bracken*'s Bay G. *Rumplefs*, 13 H. ½ I. ———	1	1
Mr. *Ball*'s Chef. M. *Mifs-Speedwell*, 13 H. 3 I. ———	2	2

LEVERPOOLE.

On the 14th of *Septemb.* a Purfe of 25 Guineas was run for at *Leverpoole*, free for fuch as never won a King's Plate; *wt.* 10 *ft.* to ent. 4 Days before running, paying 2 Guin. 2 to ftart, Stakes for the 2d beft.

This Prize was won by

	1 H.	2 H.
Sir *Richard Grofvenor*'s Chef. H. *White-Foot* ———	1	1
Mr. *Puleston*'s Chef. H. *Surley*, run on the wrong Side a Poft in the 2d Heat, and diftanc'd ———	2	*dif*
Sir *John Glyn*'s Grey M. ———	*dif*	

On

On the following Day, upon this Courſe, was 10 *l. Sterl.* for Galloways; 9 *ſt.* the higheſt give and take: to ent. 5 Days before, paying half a Guin.

	1 H.
This Prize was won by	
Mr. *Rhodes*'s Cheſ. G. *Merry-Barnaby*—	1
Sir *Tho. Fleetwood*'s Grey H.———	2

LEICESTERSHIRE, 1731.

Town of LEICESTER.

AT the Town of *Leiceſter*, on the 27th Day of *Auguſt*, a Purſe of 20 Guineas was run for; *wt.* 10 *ſt.* 1 Guin. Entr. and won by

	1 H.	2 H.
Mr. *Fleetwood*'s Brown H. *Merry-Batchelor* ———	1	1
Mr. *Bradly*'s Bay H. *Roger* ———	2	2
Mr. *Muſters*'s Bay M. *Diana*, fell juſt after ſtarting, and was diſtanc'd—	diſ	
Mr. *Wilcox*'s Grey H. *Jumping-Jerry*—	diſ	

On the following Day, on the ſame Courſe, was 10 Guin. for Galloways; 9 *ſt.* the higheſt give and take, half a Guin. Ent.

	1 H.	2 H.
The ſame was won by		
Mr. *Fleetwood*'s Roan H. *Lilliput*, 13 H. ¾ I. ———	1	1
Mr. *Coles*'s Black G. *Black-Joke*, 14 H.	2	2

A 3d and laſt Prize of this Meeting, was a free Purſe of 40 Guin. *wt.* 11 *ſt.* 3 Guin. Entr.

This

This Prize was also won by

	1 H.
Mr. *Fleetwood*'s *Merry-Batchelor* ——————	1
Mr. *Musters*'s *Diana* ———————————	2
Mr. *Plampin*'s Dun G. *White-foot* ——————	dif

Enter for all three, 16th *ditto*, and three, if insisted on, were each Day obliged to start.

MELTON-MOWBRAY.

On the 25th of *August*, a 10 *l*. Purse was run for at *Melton*, 14 Hands, to carry 9 *st*. and to give or take, if higher or lower.

Which Prize was won by	1 H.	2 H.
Mr. *Porter*'s Chesf. M. *Red-Joke*, 13 H. 2 I. ¾. ——————————————	1	1
Mr. *Bennet*'s Chesf. M. *Creeping-Molly*, 14 H. 1 I. ——————————————	3	2
Mr. *Ridgway*'s Bay G. 13 H. 3 I. ¾. ———	2	3

The 20 *l*. advertised for the foregoing Day at this Place, was not run for.

But on the 23d of *Septemb*. on this Course, the following three started for a Plate of 10 *l*. Value, *wt*. 10 *st*.

	1 H.	2 H.
Mr. *Smith*'s Grey M. *Juliana* ——————	1	1
Mr. *Parkins*'s Chesf. H. *Tickle-me-quickly* —————————————	2	2
Mr. *Gastrel*'s Chesf. G. *Single-Peeper* ———	3	3

LUT-

LUTTERWORTH.

On the 5th Day of *October*, a Purse of 25 Guin. was run for at *Lutterworth*; wt. 12 *st.* and the Winner to be sold for 50 Guineas: 2 Guin. Entr.

This Prize was won by	1 H.	2 H.
Mr. *How's* Bay H. *King's-Fisher*———	1	1
Mr. *Coles's* Chef. M. *Peggy-grieves-me*—	2	2
Mr. *Brewster's* Chef. H. *Club-Foot* ——	3	3

On the following Day, on the same Course, was 10 Guineas for Galloways; 9 *st.* the highest give and take: 1 Guin. Entr.

This Prize was won by	1 H.	2 H.
Mr. *Coles's* Black G. *Black-Joke*, 14 H.	1	1
Sir *Arthur Haslerige's* Bay M. 13 H. 3 I. ¼.———	2	2
Mr. *Munday's* Bay G. 13 H. 3 I. ½. ——	3	dif
Mr. *Smith's* Brown G. 13 H. ½ I.———	dif	

Enter for each Prize respectively, 7 Days before running.

※※※※※※※※ ※※※ ※※※ ※※※

LINCOLNSHIRE, 1731.

STAMFORD.

ON the 10th Day of *March*, upon this Course, Mr. *Cumberland*'s Grey M. *Charming-Jenny*, beat Mr. *Game*'s Chef. M. *Panther*; 12 ft. 4 m. 20 Guineas.

On the 8th Day of *June*, upon the same Course, a Plate of 40 l. Value was run for, free only for six Year Olds; 3 Guin. Entr. for which, had one only started, he must have pd 10 Guin. towards the next Year's Plate: but there started for the same the three following.

	1 H.	2 H.
Mr. *Rich*'s Bay H. *Huffar* ———	1	1
Mr. *Hardy*'s Bay G. *Surly* ———	2	2
Mr. *Mackworth*'s Grey H. *Favourite* —	3	3

A 2d Prize of this Meeting was 20 Guineas, for Galloways, 9 ft. the highest give and take, 2 Guin. Entr. if but one starts, to pay 7 Guineas towards the next Year's Plate; which Prize was won by

	1 H.	2 H.
Sir *Arthur Haflerige*'s Bay M. *Ring-tail*, 13 H. 2 I. ———	1	1
Mr. *Fleetwood*'s Roan H. *Lilliput*, 13 H. 1 I. ¼ ———	2	2

On

On the 10th *ditto*, upon this Course, the free
Purse of 80 Guineas, was run for, *wt.* 10 ft. 5
Guineas Entr. If but one enters for this Prize, to
have his Entrance-Money return'd, 10 Guineas allow'd for Charges, *&c.* and the said Prize not run
for: But there started for the same, the eight following;

	1 H.	2 H.	3 H.
Duke of *Ancaster*'s Grey H. *Gentleman*	1	3	1
Mr. *Musters*'s Bay M. *Diana*	4	1	3
Mr. *Bright*'s Brown M. *Emma*	2	4	2
Mr. *Brewster*'s Bay M. *Miss Nesham*	3	2	dif
Mr. *Fleetwood*'s Bay H. *Eaton*	5	dr.	
Mr. *Leathes*'s Chef. H. *White-Stockings*, lam'd and distanc'd	dif		
Mr. *Coles*'s Brown H. *Whitefoot*	dif		
Mr. *Turner*'s Bay H. *Roger*	dif		

The last Prize of this Meeting, was 20 Guineas
for such as never won 5 Guineas, *wt.* 12 ft. 2 Guin.
Entr. and won by

	1 H.		
Mr. *Brewster*'s Chef. H. *Catch-him-that-can*	1		
Mr. *Anderson*'s Chef. G. *Crutches*	2		

TATHWELL.

On the 10th Day of *March*, upon this Course,
Mr. *Ascough*'s Grey G. *Merry-Harrier*, beat Mr.
Chaplain's Grey M. *Prophetess*, 12 ft. 4 Miles, 20
Guineas.

BEMBROOKE.

On the 1st of *April*, upon this Course, Mr. *Heneage*'s Chef. M. beat Mr. *Hildyard*'s Chef. M. 8 ft.
4 Miles, 10 Guineas.   1   And

And also, on the same Day and Course, Mr. *Newton*'s Roan G. *Rumbler*, beat Mr. *White*'s Bay G. *Grains*; 13 *st*. 7 *l*. 4 Miles, 20 Guineas.

KIRTON.

On the 3d Day of *May*, upon this Course, Mr. *Fitzwilliams*'s Bay M. 13 H. 2 I. ½; Mr. *Broughton*'s Grey M. 13 H. 2 I. ½; and Mr. *Morly*'s Bay G. 13 H. 2 I. ¼, to run one 4 Miles Heat, for 20 Guineas each, 50 of which to be the Prize of the first, and the other 10 the Prize of the 2d. Their Places were as follow,

The Bay M. ——————————— 1
The Grey ——————————— 2
The Gelding ——————————— 3

The Gelding had won the 50 Guineas, but he run out of the Course, and against a Wall, yet came in 2d, but the Rider omitted to prove his Weight, which gave the Grey M. a Title to the 10 Guineas.

On the 4th Day of *October*, upon this Course Mr. *Kirk*'s Bay M. 11 *st*. beat Mr. *Fitzwilliams*'s Dun M. 10 *st*. 4 Miles, 45 Guineas.

BOSTON.

On the 22d of *June*, a 30 *l*. Purse was run for at *Boston*, free only for five Year Olds, *wt*. 10 *st*. 3 Guineas Entr.

	1 H.	2 H.
This Prize was won by		
Lady *Chaplin*'s Brown H. *Spot* ——	1	1
Mrs. *Rawson*'s Black H. *Smiling-Tom*	2	2

On the following Day, upon the same Course, was 10 Guineas, for Galloways, 9 *st*. the highest

H   give

give and take, one Guinea Entr. and the Winner to be fold for 20 Guineas.

	1 H.	2 H.	3 H.
This Prize was won by			
Mr. *White*'s Bay M. *Sweet-lips*, 13 H. ¼ I.	1	1	1
Mr. *Bafs*'s Bay M. *Charming-Jenny*, 13 H. 3 I.	2	2	2
Mr. *Weaver*'s Chef. M. *She'as-Loft-her-fweet-Maidenhead*, 14 H.	4	3	dr.
Mr. *Bradley*'s Roan G. *Partner*, 13 H. 1 I. ½	3	dr.	

On the fame Courfe, on the 24th *ditto*, a 20 *l*. Purfe was run for, *wt*. 10 *ft*. and the Winner to be fold for 40 Guineas ; which Prize was won by

	1 H.	2 H.
Mr. *Heneage*'s Bay H. *White-nofe*	1	1
Mr. *Ward*'s Chef. G. *Carlifle*	3	2
Mr. *Thatcher*'s Bay M. *Fair-Rofamond*	2	dif
Mr. *Hall*'s Chef. M. *Smiling-Jenny*	dif	
Mr. *Afhley*'s Bay G. *Kifs-in-a-Corner*	dif	
Mr. *Bennet*'s Bay G. *Scar*	dif	

The laft Prize of this Meeting, was a 40 *l*. Purfe on the following Day, *wt*. 12 *ft*. and the Winner to be fold for 80 Guineas.

	1 H.	2 H.
This Prize was won by		
Sir *Arthur Hafterige*'s Chef. G. *Whitefoot*	1	1
Mr. *Grifewood*'s Brown H. *Cripple*	3	2
Mr. *Garthfide*'s Chef. G. *Fox-hunter*	2	3

SPALDEN.

About the middle of the Seafon, a Purfe of 15 *l*. Sterling, was run for at *Spalden*, *wt*. 10 *ft*. and won by

Mr.

	1 H.	2 H.
Mr. *Bennet*'s Bay G. *Who's-afraid* ——	1	1
Mr. *James*'s Grey G. *Coniack* ——————	2	2

On the following Day, upon this Course, was 10 *l.* for Galloways, 9 *ſt.* the higheſt give and take, and won by

	1 H.
Mr. *Weaver*'s Cheſ. M. *Favourite* ——	1
Mr. *Trout*'s Bay G. ————————	*diſ*
Mr. *Bingham*'s Cheſ. M. *Pretty-Betty*	*diſ*

On the following Day, upon the ſame Courſe, a Purſe of 25 *l.* Sterling, was run for, *wt.* 10 *ſt.* and alſo won by

	1 H.	2 H.
Mr. *Bennet*'s Bay G. *Who's-afraid* ———	1	1
Mr. *Ward*'s Cheſ. G. *Carliſle* ———————	2	2
Mr. *Harwood*'s Grey M. ————————	*diſ*	

GAINSBOROUGH.

On the 25th Day of *Auguſt*, a Purſe of 15 *l.* Sterling was run for at *Gainsborough*, free only for ſuch as never won 20 *l.* 14 Hands, to carry 9 *ſt.* and to give or take, if higher or lower.

	1 H.	2 H.	3 H.
This Prize was won by			
Mr. *Simkins*'s Bay G. *Poſt-Boy*, 13 H. 3 I. ———————	1	1	
Mr. *Wharton*'s Grey G. *Have-at-ye*, 14 H. 1 I. $\frac{1}{4}$ ———————	2	2	1
Mr. *Render*'s Bay M. *Strong-Beer*, 13 H. 3 I. $\frac{1}{4}$ ———————	3	3	*diſ*

On the following Day, upon this Course, a Purse of 20 *l.* Cash was run for, free only for such as never won above 50 *l.* *wt.* 11 *st.* and won by

	1 H.	2 H.
Mr. *Goostry's* Grey M. *Derbyshire-Sally*	1	1
Mr. *Wrigglesworth's* Bay H. *Bay-Manton*	2	2
Mr. *Wharton's* Have-at-ye ————	dis	

On the 27th *ditto*, on the same Course, was 10 *l.* Cash for Galloways, 9 *st.* the highest give and take, and also won by

	1 H.	2 H.
Mr. *Simkins's* Post Boy———————	1	1
Mr. *Walker's* Grey M. *Diana,* 13 H. 2 I. ¼————	2	2
Mr. *Morly's* Bay G. *Will-if-he-can,* 13 H. 3 I.———	3	3
Mr. *Fitzwilliams's* Dun M. *Hormza,* 13 H. 2 I. ¾———	dis	

GRANTHAM.

On the 28th Day of *September,* a 20 *l.* Plate was run for here, free only for such as never won 10 *l.* *wt.* 12 *st.* one Guinea Entr. which Entrance-Money goes towards raising the next Year's Plate.

This Prize was won by

	1 H.	2 H.
Lord *Haversham's* Ches. M. *Bloxham-Betty* —————	1	1
Lord *Hamilton's* Black H. *Country-Dick*	2	2

Upon this Course the following Day, was a 10 *l.* Plate for Galloways, 9 *st.* the highest give and take, half a Guinea Entr. and the Winner to be sold for 20 Guineas.

This

This Prize was won by	1 H.
Mr. *Porter's* Chef. M. *Red-joke*, 13 H. 2 I. ¾	1
Mr. *Birch's* Grey G. *Merry-Lad*, 14 H.	dif

On the 30th *ditto*, upon this Courfe, a Plate of 20 *l.* value was run for, being the Prefent of Sir *Michael Newton*, Knt. of the Bath, and Reprefentative in Parliament for this Corporation of *Grantham*: This Prize is call'd a Whim or whimfical Plate, becaufe the Conditions of running for the fame, are different from thofe of all other Prizes; the Entrance-Money is one Guinea and a Half, which Money is the Prize of the 2d beft.

Horfes, &c. ftarting for this Prize carry, if 7 Years Old or upwards, 10 ft; thofe of 6 Years Old, 9 ft. 7 l.; thofe of 5 Years Old, 8 ft. 11 l.; thofe of 4 Year Olds, 8 ft. and the Horfe, &c. that wins the 1ft Heat, is entitled to the Plate, and the others (if others there are) ftart a 2d Heat for the Stakes. Thofe that ftarted for the fame, and their Places, are as follows;

	1 H.	2 H.
Mr. *Dighton's* Grey M. 5 Years Old —	1	
Mr. *Bennet's* Bay G. *Who's-afraid,* 6 Years Old	2	1
Ld *Haverfham's* Chef. M. *Bloxham-Betty,* 6 Years Old	{3	2
Duke of *Ancaster's* Grey H. *Surly,* 4 Years Old	dif	
Sir *Michael Newton's* Brown H. *Quiet,* full aged.	dif	

ALFORD.

On the 20th Day of *October*, a Purfe of 15 Guin. was run for at *Alford*, wt. 10 ft. and the Winner

to be fold for 25 Guineas; to enter on the 13th
ult. paying one Guinea and a half.

This Prize was won by	1 H.	2 H.
Mr. *Bennet's* Bay G. *Who's-afraid*	1	1
Mr. *Gaffet's* Chef. G.	3	2
Mr. *Porter's* Chef. M. *Diana*	2	3

On the fame Courfe, on the following Day, was
10 Guineas for Galloways, 9 ft. the highest give
and take; the Winner to be fold for 15 Guineas,
to enter on the 14th *ditto*, paying one Guinea.

This Prize was won by	1 H.	2 H.
The above-nam'd *Diana*, 13 H. 2 I. ¾	1	1
Mr. *Heneage's* Bay G. *Laft-Time-of asking*	2	2
Mr. *Hildyard's* Grey M. fell and	dif	

On the 22d *ditto*, upon this Courfe, a Prize,
confifting of 25 Guineas, and call'd the Lady's Plate,
was run for; this Prize was free only for fuch 5
Year Olds as never won a Plate, *wt.* 9 ft. and the
Winner to be fold for 60 Guineas: To enter on
the 16th *ditto*, paying 2 Guineas.

This Prize was won by	1 H.	2 H.
Mr. *Parkins's* Bay G. *Tickle-me-quickly*	1	1
Mr. *Humberftone's* Grey H. *Blue-Ribbon*	3	2
Mr. *Jackfon's* Bay H. *Fortunatus*	2	3

For either of thefe Prizes any might enter at
the Poft, paying double; and 3 for each Prize were
oblig'd to ftart.

MID-

⚜⚜⚜⚜⚜⚜⚜⚜⚜⚜⚜⚜

MIDDLESEX, 1751.

HAMPSTEAD.

ON the 2d of *June*, a Purse of 15 Guineas was run for at *Hampstead*, free only for such as never won 25 Guineas, 14 Hands, to carry 10 st. and to give or take, if higher or lower; which Prize was won by

	1 H.	2 H.	3 H.
Mr. *Grandy's* Bay G. *Squirrel*, 14 H. ¼ I.	1	1	1
Mr. *Wans's* Brown M. 13 H. ¼ I.	2	2	2
Mr. *Clark's* Brown H. *Fear-not*, 14 H. 1 I.	dif		
Mr. *Pierce's* Sorrel G. 13 H. 1 I.	dif		

On the same Course, upon the Day following, was 10 Guineas, for Galloways, 9 st. the highest give and take, and won by

	1 H.	2 H.
Mr. *Archer's* Bay M. *Lincolnshire-Lady*, 13 H. 3 I.	1	1
Mr. *Clark's* Grey M. *Miss-Maggot*, 14 H.	2	2
Mr. *Bonas's* Brown H. *Black-Legs*, 14 H.	dif	

In the Month of *September*, upon this Course, a give and take Plate of 10 *l*. value was run for; which Prize was won by

Mr.

	1 H.	2 H.
Mr. *Lewis*'s Chef. G. *Cripple* ————	1	1
Mr. *Dean*'s Grey G. ————	2	2
Mr. *Symonds*'s Black H. ————	dif	

On the following Day, on the same Course, was a 10 *l.* Plate, for Galloways, 9 *ft.* the highest give and take, and won by

	1 H.	2 H.	3 H.
Ld *Hamilton*'s Grey M. *Northern-Nancy*, 13 H. 2 l. ————	1	1	1
Mr. *Bonas*'s Bay H. *Black-Legs*, 14 H.	2	2	3
Mr. *Flanders*'s Bay M. *Miss-Prue*, 13 H. 2 l. ————	3	3	2
Mr. *Smith*'s Grey H. ————	dif		

HOUNSLOW.

On the 16th Day of *June*, a Purse of 30 Guin. was run for at *Hounslow*, wt. 11 *ft.* Entr. 3 Guin. or 5 at the Post.

	1 H.	2 H.
This Prize was won by		
Mr. *Sheppard*'s Bay G. *Stay-till-I-come* ————	1	1
Mr. *Coles*'s Grey M. *Painted-Lady* —	2	2
Mr. *Baynes*'s Black G. *Magpye* ————	3	3
Mr. *Rich*'s Bay H. ————	4	4
Mr. *Adams*'s Bay G. *Fine-bones* ———	5	5

On the same Course, the following Day, was 10 *l.* for Galloways, 9 *ft.* the highest give and take, Entr. one Guinea, or 2 at the Post; and won by

	1 H.	2 H.	3 H.
Mr. *Bonas*'s Brown H. *Tom-Tit*, 13 H. 3 l. ¾ ½ q. ————	1	1	1

Mr.

	1 H.	2 H.	3 H.
Mr. *Tredway*'s Chef. M. *Brick-duff*, 13 H. 3 I. ———	3	2	2
Mr. *Dainty*'s Bay M. *Uncertain*, 13 H. 3 I. ¼ ½ q. ———	2	3	dr.
Mr. *Leake*'s Bay M. 13 H. 2 I. ———	dif		

This Mare of Mr. *Leake*'s came in firft the firft Heat, but fhe run on the wrong Side a Poft, which of courfe render'd her diftanc'd.

On the 18th *ditto*, on the fame Courfe, was a 20 l. for Hunters, *wt*. 12 ft. Entr. 2 Guineas, or 4 at the Poft.

	1 H.	2 H.
This Prize was won by		
Mr. *Gill*'s Bay G. *Plain-Dealer* ———	1	1
Mr. *Sharp*'s Chef. G. *Lady-Legs* ———	2	2
Mr. *Hoskins*'s Bay G. *Fox-hunter* ———	3	3
Mr. *Longbottom*'s Chef. G. *Fugger* ———	4	4
Mr. *Chapman*'s Grey M. *Who-can-tell*	dif	
Mr. *Brown*'s Sorrel H. *Sloven* ———	dif	

Upon this Courfe, on the 20th of *October*, was a 10 l. Plate, for Galloways, 13 H. 2 I. to carry 7 ft. 7 l. if lower, to be allow'd Weight for Inches.

	1 H.	2 H.
This Prize was won by		
Mr. *Flanders*'s Bay M. *Miss-Prue* ———	1	1
Sir *Robert Fagg*'s Bay H. *Bully* ———	2	2
Mr. *Robinson*'s Chef. G. *Marble* ———	dif	

HACKNEY-MARSH.

On the 17th Day of *August*, a 10 l. Plate was run for at *Hackney-Marsh*, 14 Hands, to carry 9 ft. and to give or take, if higher or lower.

This

This Prize was won by

	1 H.	2 H.
Mr. *Griffin*'s Grey M. *Country-Kate*, 14 H. 1 I. ½ ———	1	1
Mr. *Woodman*'s Black M. *Creeping-Kate*, 14 H. ½ I. ———	2	2
Mr. *Busby*'s Grey G. *Stay-till-I-come*, 14 H. ———	3	3
Mr. *Bedow*'s Bay M. *How-can-you-tell*, 14 H. ———	4	4

. On the fame Courfe, on the 21ft *ditto*, a Plate of the fame value, was run for, *wt.* alfo the fame, and won by

	1 H.	2 H.
The fame Mare of Mr. *Griffin*'s ———	1	1
Mr. *Lawrence*'s Black G. *Stay till-I-come*, 13 H. 3 I. ———	3	2
Mr. *Mafon*'s Chef. H. *Wanton-Billy*, 14 H. 1 I. ———	2	3
Mr. *Woodman*'s Grey M. *Diana*, 14 H.	dif	

Upon this Courfe, on the 7th of *September*, a Plate of 12 *l.* value was run for, *wt.* 10 *ß.* and won by

	1 H.	2 H.
Mr. *Woodman*'s Black M. *Creeping-Kate*	1	1
Mr. *Bonas*'s Brown H. *Black-Legs* ———	2	2

On the 15th Day of *October*, on the fame Courfe, a 2d 12 *l.* Plate was run for, 14 Hands, to carry 9 *ß.* and to give or take, if higher or lower; which Prize was won by

	1 H.	2 H.
Mr. *Griffin*'s Grey M. *Country-Kate*, 14 H. 1 I. ½ ———	1	1

Ld

	1 H.	2 H.
Ld *Hamilton*'s Grey M. *Northern-Nancy*, 13 H. 2 I.	2	2
Mr. *Woodman*'s Black M. *Creeping-Kate*, 14 H. 1/2	3	3

MONMOUTHSHIRE, 1731.

Town of MONMOUTH.

ON the 14th Day of *September*, a 30 *l.* Plate was run for at *Monmouth*, *wt.* 11 *st.* to enter the *Friday* before, paying 2 Guineas.

	1 H.	2 H.
This Prize was won by		
Mr. *Coles*'s Chef. M. *Peggy-grieves-me*	1	1
Mr. *Kirby*'s Bay G. *Nicholina*	2	dr.
Mr. *Mackworth*'s Grey H. *Fear-not*	3	dr.

On the following Day, upon this Course, a 10 *l.* Plate was run for, *wt.* 10 *st.* to enter the same Day, paying Half a Guinea.

	1 H.	2 H.
This Prize was won by		
Mr. *Kirby*'s Bay G. *Nicholina*	1	1
Mr. *Bathurst*'s Bay M.	2	2
Mr. *Jones*'s Bay G. *Come-Rogue*	dif	
Mr. *Jack*'s Chef. M.	dif	

On the 8th *ditto*, on the same Course, was a 20 *l.* Plate, for Galloways, 10 *st.* the highest give and take, and won by

Mr.

	1 H.	2 H.
Mr. *Hurst*'s Bay G. *Squirrel*, 14 H. ———	1	1
Mr. *Prichard*'s Bay G. *Now-or-never*, 13H.	3	2
Capt. *Keymeff*'s Brown H. *Dolphin*, 13 H. 3 I. ¼ ———	2	3

❋❋❋❋❋❋❋❋❋❋❋❋

NORFOLK, 1731.

HOLT.

ON the 27th of *July*, a Purse of 20 Guin. was run for at *Holt*, 14 Hands, to carry 9 *st.* and to give or take, if higher or lower: 2 Guin. Entr.

	1 H.	2 H.	3 H.
This Prize was won by			
Mr. *Tuting*'s Brown M. *Cynder-Wench*, 14 H. ¼ I. ———	2	1	1
Mr. *Ireland*'s Chef. M. *Venus*, 14 H. ¼ I. ———	1	2	2

On the fame Course, on the following Day, a Plate of 10 Guin. Value was run for, being for Galloways, 9 *st.* the highest give and take: one Guin. Entr.

	1 H.	
This Prize was won by		
Mr. *Johnson*'s Brown H. *Stay-till-I-come*, 13 H. 2 I. ¼ ———	1	
Mr. *Brown*'s Grey M. *Blooming-Betty*, 13 H. 2 I. ¾ ———	2	

Mr.

Mr. *Seal's* Sorrel M. *Mutton-Pye-Moll*, 13. H. 3 I. ¼.	*dif*
Mr. *Earl's* Sorrel M. *Cumberland-Kitty*, 14 H.	*dif*

On the 28th *ditto*, on the fame Courfe, a free Purfe of 30 Guin. was run for; *wt.* 11*ft.* 3 Guin. Entr.

	1 H.
Which Prize was won by	
Mr. *Tuting's* Brown M. *Welch-Lady*	1
Mr. *Briggs's* Grey M. *Small-Hopes*	*dif*

The 26th *ditto* was Entrance-Day for all thefe Prizes, or at the Poft for either, paying double.

Had but one ftarted for either, he muft have p^d one 3d of the fame towards the next Year's Plates.

NORTHAMPTONSHIRE, 1731.

DAVENTRY.

ON the 14th of *July*, a Plate of 15 *l.* Value was run for at *Daventry*; *wt.* 10 *ft.* and the Winner to be fold for 30 Guin. 1 Guin. Entr.

	1 H.	2 H.	3 H.
Which Prize was won by			
Mr. *Woodman's* Grey H. *Sly*	1	2	1
Mr. *Clark's* Brown H.	5	1	2
Mr. *Worfley's* Chef. H. *Smiling-Ball*	3	3	3
Mr. *Ward's* Chef. G. *Merry-Batchelor*	2	4	4
Sir *Arthur Haflerige's* Chef. H. *Who-can-tell*	4	*dif*	
Mr. *Tuting's* Bay H. *Squirrel*	*dif*		

I

On the same Course, the following Day, a Purse of 40 Guin. was run for, free only for such as never started before; *wt.* 12 *st.* and the Winner to be sold for 40 Guin.

This Prize was won by	1 H.	2 H.
Mr. *Green*'s Chef. H. *Traveller* ———	1	1
Mr. *Neal*'s Black H. *Sloven* ———	3	2
Earl of *Hallifax*'s Bay H. *Bay-Colt*——	2	dr.
Mr. *Knightly*'s Chef. G. *Foxhunter*——	dif	

Upon this Course, on the 16th *ditto*, was 10 Guin. for Galloways; 9 *st.* the highest give and take: one Guin. Entr. and won by

	1 H.	2 H.
Mr. *Porter*'s M. *Red-Joke*, 13 H. 3 I.—	1	1
Mr. *Hide*'s Strawberry G. *Strawberry*, 13 H. 3 I.———	2	2
Mr. *Knightly*'s Chef. H. *Turtle-Dove*, 13 H. 3 I.———	3	3
Mr. *Neal*'s Bay M. *Cripple*, 13 H. 3 I. $\frac{1}{4}$, fell lame in the first Heat ———	4	dr.
Mr. *Stratford*'s Chef. M. *Single-Peeper*, 13 H. 3 I. ———	dif	
Mr. *Quin*'s Chef. M. *Dumplin*, 13 H. 2 I.	dif	

Enter for the two first of these Prizes, on the *Thursday*, and for the third, on the Day next before running.

On the 20th of *August*, upon this Course, Mr. *Artup*'s Bay G. *Bay-Robin*, beat Mr. *Marriot*'s White G. *Smoker*; each rode by the Proprietor, 10 Miles, 11 Guin. and 14 Shillings.

City

City of PETERBOROUGH.

On the 17th Day of *August*, a Purse of 20 Guin. was run for at *Peterborough*, free only for such Hunters as never won a Purse or Plate; *wt.* 12 *st.* and the Winner to be sold for 40 Guineas, 2 Guin. Entr.

	1 H.	2 H.
This Prize was won by		
Mr. *Pelham*'s Brown G. *Foxhunter*———	1	1
Mr. *Game*'s Chef. G. *Smiling-Billy*———	2	2

On the following Day, upon this Course, was a 10 *l.* Plate, for such Galloways as never won 10 *l.* 9 *st.* the highest give and take; the Winner to be sold for 10 Guineas.

	1 H.	2 H.
Which Plate was won by		
Mr. *Cumberland*'s Grey H. *Merry-Batchelor*, 13 H. 3 I.———	1	1
Mr. *Quince*'s Chef. G. *Pity-me-now*—	3	2
Mr. *Rock*'s Grey M. *Peggy-grieves-me*—	2	3
Mr. *Williamson*'s Grey H. *Robin* ———	dif	
Mr. *Eaton*'s Grey G. *Small-Hopes*———	dif	
Mr. *Hall*'s Roan G. ———	dif	

On the 19th *ditto*, on the same Course, a free Plate of 30 *l.* Value was run for; *wt.* 10 *st.* but the Winner to be sold for 60 Guin. 3 Guin. Entr.

	1 H.	2 H.	3 H.
This Prize was won by the			
Earl of *Portmore*'s Grey H. *Spot*———	3	1	1
Mr. *Jones*'s Chef. M. *Sweetest-when-naked* ———	2	dif	2
Earl of *Hallifax*'s Chef. H. *Squirrel*—	1	dif	

KETTERING.

On the 31ſt Day of *Auguſt*, a 10 *l*. Plate was run for at *Kettering*, free for Galloways, 9 *ſt*. the higheſt give and take: the Winner to be ſold for 15 Guin.

	1 H.	2 H.
This Prize was won by		
Mr. *Thompſon*'s Cheſ. M. *Red-Joke*, 13 H. 3 I. ——————	1	1
Mr. *Hint*'s Dun G. *Small-Hopes*, 13 H. 3 I. ——————	2	2
Mr. *Holland*'s Grey G. *Smiling-Tom*, 13 H. 3 I. ——————	3	3

On the following Day, on the ſame Courſe, a 20 *l*. Plate was run for, free for any that never won above 30 *l*. *wt*. 10 *ſt*. and won by

	1 H.	2 H.
Mr. *Eyres*'s Cheſ. G. *Single-Peeper* ————	1	1
Mr. *Wilcox*'s Grey H. *Tantivy* ————	2	2
Mr. *Baynes*'s Black G. *Scare-Crow* ————	3	3

Town of NORTHAMPTON.

On the 22d Day of *Septemb.* a 15 *l*. Plate was run for at *Northampton*; *wt*. 10 *ſt*. and the Winner to be ſold for 30 *l*. 30 *s*. Entr.

	1 H.	2 H.
Which Prize was won by		
Mr. *Coles*'s Grey M. *Small-Hopes* ————	1	1
Sir *Roger Burgain*'s Bay G. *Red-Cap* ————	3	2
Mr. *Clark*'s Brown H. *Fear-nothing* ———	2	3

On the follpwing Day, upon the ſame Courſe, was a 15 *l*. Plate for Galloways; 9 *ſt*. the higheſt give and take: 30 *s*. Entr. and the Winner alſo to be ſold for 30 *l*.   Which

Which Prize was won by the same	1 H.	2 H.
Mr. *Coles*'s Black G. *Little-Esquire* ——	1	1
Mr. *Inkes*'s Bay M. *Jenny-Tight* ——	3	2
Mr. *Webster*'s Grey M. *Filting-Peggy* ——	2	dr.
Mr. *Russel*'s Bay M. *Moll-Frisky* ——	dif	

On the 24th *ditto*, on the same Course, a 40 *l.* Plate was run for, free only for such as never won above 50 Guineas; *wt.* 12 *st.* 3 Guin. Entr.

This Prize was won by	1 H.	2 H.	3 H.
Sir *Humph. Monoux*'s Dun G. *Fox-hunter* ——————— }	4	1	1
Mr. *How*'s Bay H. *King's-Fisher* ——	1	4	2
Mr. *Thatcher*'s Bay M. *Fair-Rosamond*	2	2	3
Ld Visc. *How*'s Bay G. *Capt. Frisky*—	3	3	dr.
Mr. *Pelham*'s Brown G. *Wry-Neck*—	dif		

Enter for each of these Prizes on the *Saturday* before. Had but one started for either, he must have pd one 3d of the Value of the same towards the next Year's Plate.

NORTHUMBERLAND, 1731.

HEXHAM.

ON the 10th Day of *May*, a 10 *l.* Plate was run for at *Hexham*, free only for 5 Year Olds, *wt.* 9 *ft.* to enter on the 29th of *April*, paying 15 *s.*

This Prize was won by	1H.	2H.	3H.
Mr. *Solesby*'s Grey M. *Jenny-Nettle*	1	1	2
Mr. *Wood*'s Bay H. *Thro'-the-Woods-Laddy*	2	2	1
Mr. *Charlton*'s Grey M. *Small-Hopes*	3	3	3
Mr. *Friend*'s Bay M. *Aldon-Peggy*	4	4	dr.
Mr. *Gibson*'s Bay G. *Now-or-never*	dif		

On the same Course, on the 7th *ditto*, a free Plate of 12 *l.* Value was run for; *wt.* 10 *ft.* to ent. on the 1ft *ditto*, pay one Guin. and half.

Which Prize was won by	1H.	2H.
Mr. *Fenwick*'s Grey G. *Smock-Face*	1	1
Mr. *Wilson*'s Chef. M. *Goldfinch*	2	2
Mr. *Lambert*'s Bay G. *Thro'-the-Woods-Laddy*	dif	

BERWICK UPON TWEED.

On the 18th Day of *May*, a Prize of 15 Guineas Value was run for at *Berwick*, free only for such as never ftarted for 15 Guin. *wt.* 10 *ft.* exclusive of Bridle and Saddle: Ent. 1 Guin. and half, and three to ftart.

This

This Prize was won by	1 H.	2 H.	3 H.
Mr. *Lifle*'s Bay M. *Miss-Kitty* ————	6	1	1
Mr. *Nelfon*'s Grey M. ————	3	2	dif
Mr. *Fenwick*'s Cream-colour'd M. ——	1	dif	
Mr. *Wilkey*'s Dun G. ————	2	dif	
Mr. *Carr*'s Bay G. *Sloven* ————	4	dif	
Mr. *Jeffry*'s Grey H. ————	5	dif	

On the fame Courfe, on the following Day, was a 10 *l*. Plate for Galloways; 9 *ft*. the higheft give and take : 4 to ftart, and 1 Guin. Entr.

This Prize was won by	1 H.	2 H.	3 H.
Mr. *Story*'s Chef. G. ————	2	1	1
Mr. *Stonerig*'s Grey G. ————	1	2	2
Mr. *Swinburn*'s Grey G. ————	3	dif	
Mr. *Younghusband*'s Chef. M. ——	dif		

NEWCASTLE UPON TYNE.

On the 14th of *June*, the Meeting began at *New-caftle upon Tyne*; the Prize of which Day was a Plate of 30 *l*. Value, free only for fuch as were not more than 3 Lunar Months over 5 Years old; *wt*. 9 *ft*. 2 Miles at a Heat : 4 to ftart, and 2 Guin. Entr.

If in running for this Prize, three diftinct Horfes, *&c*. win each one a Heat, that which wins the 3d Heat is intitled to the fd Prize, without ftarting a 4th Heat.

This Prize was won by	1 H.	2 H.	3 H.
Mr. *Smales*'s Bay H. *Young-Thirkeld*, got by *Swallow* ————	7	5	1
Mr. *Errington*'s Bay H. *Doborucki* ——	2	1	3
Mr. *Elftob*'s Chef. M. *Lucy* ————	1	6	dif
Duke of *Bolton*'s Grey M. *Mary-Grey*	3	3	2

Mr.

	1 H.	2 H.	3 H.
Mr. *Cook*'s Grey H. *Sober-Cuddy* ——	5	4	4
Mr. *Crefwell*'s Grey M. *Victory* ——	6	2	7
Mr. *Graham*'s Bay M. *Brown-Betty* ——	4	7	5
Mr. *Ellifon*'s Chef. M. *Peevifh* ——	9	8	
Mr. *Brown*'s Black G. *Blackbird* ——	8		

On the Day following, on the fame Courfe, a
10 *l.* Plate was run for, free only for Tradefmens
Horfes of this Town of *Newcaftle*; 14 Hands, to
carry 10 *ft.* and to give or take, if higher or lower.

	1 H.	2 H.	3 H.
This Prize was won by			
Mr. *Gibfon*'s Chef. M. *Smiling-Kitty*	1	1	2
Mr. *Armorer*'s Chef. M. *Small-Hopes*	5	2	1
Mr. *Humble*'s Ch. G. *Little-thought-of*	2	3	3
Mr. *Clifton*'s Grey M. *Little-thought-of*	3	dif	
Mr. *Selby*'s G. *Surly* —— ——	4	dif	
Mr. *Myddleton*'s Chef. M. *Flower-in-May* ——	6	dif	
Mr. *Blenkinfop*'s Bay G. *Bolder-than ever* —— ——	7	dif	
Mr. *Harrifon*'s Grey G. *Commodore* ——	8	dr.	
Mr. *Smith*'s Black G. *Black-John* ——	dif		
Mr. *Dawfon*'s Grey M. *Wafp* ——	dif		
Mr. *Smith*'s Chef. G. *Crutches* ——	dif		

On the fame Courfe, on the following Day, was
20 Guineas for Galloways; 10 *ft.* the higheft give
and take, 4 to ftart, and one Guin. and a half Entr.

	1 H.	2 H.	3 H.
This Prize was won by			
Mr. *Hartford*'s Grey H. *Spot*, 14 H. ——	1	1	2
Mr. *Stevenfon*'s Chef. M. *Mifs-Stevenfon*, 14 H. —— ——	2	3	1

Mr.

	1 H.	2 H.	3 H.
Mr. *Blacket*'s Bay G. *Bold-Thirkeld*, 13 H. ¾.——————	3	2	3
Mr. *White*'s Grey M. *Smiling-Betty*, 14 H.——————	dis		

A fourth Prize of this Meeting, was the Gold Cup of 50 Guin. Value, free only for such as were not more than three Lunar Months over six Years old ; *wt.* 10 st. 3 to start, and 3 Guin. Entr.

	1 H.	2 H.
This Prize was won by		
Mr. *Smith*'s Bay M. *Smiling-Molly*——————	1	1
Mr. *Bowes*'s Black H. *Buck*——————	5	2
Sir *John Swinburn*'s Grey M. *Sweet-Lips*	2	3
Mr. *Nesham*'s Bay H. *Chevalier*——————	3	dis
Mr. *Creswell*'s Grey M. *Frosty-Face*——————	4	dis

A fifth and last Prize of this Meeting, was a free Plate of 40 l. Value; *wt.* 10 st. 4 to start, and 50 s. Entr.

	1 H.	2 H.	3 H.	4 H.
This Prize was won by				
Mr. *Smith*'s Grey H. *Secretary*, often call'd *Midge* ——————	2	2	1	1
Sir *William Middleton*'s Chef. H. *Scipio*——————	3	1	2	2
Mr. *Fenwick*'s Bay H. *Wanton-Willy*——————	1	3	dr.	
Mr. *Barrow*'s Grey H. *Rusty*——————	dis			

Enter for all five, on the *Saturday* before running.

ALNWICK.

On the 13th Day of *July*, a 20 l. Plate was run for at *Alnwick*, free only for such as were not more than

than 4 Lunar Months over five Years old; *wt.* 10 *ft.*
2 Miles at a Heat, 2 Guin. Entr.

This Prize was won by	1 H.	2 H.
Mr. *Solesby*'s Grey M. *Jenny-Nettle* ——	1	1
Mr. *Charlton*'s Grey M. ————	2	2
Mr. *Clarke*'s Grey M. ————	dif	
Mr. *Carr*'s Grey G. ————	dif	

On the same Day and Course, a Plate of 10 *l.* Value was run for, free only for such as were not more than 4 Lunar Months over 4 Years old; *wt.* 9 *ft.* 1 Guin. Entr.

This Prize was won by	1 H.
Mr. *Cowling*'s Chef. M. *White-Nose* ——	1
Mr. *Hutchinson*'s Black M. ————	2
Mr. *Grey*'s Bay M. ————	3
Mr. *Robinson*'s Bay M. ————	4

On the following Day, on the same Course, was a 10 Guin. Purse for Galloways; 10 *ft.* the higheft give and take, half a Guin. Entr. Stakes for the 2d beft. This Prize was a Prefent to the Town from the Right Hon. the Ld *Offulften*, and won by

	1 H.	2 H.	3 H.
Mr. *Armftrong*'s Bay M. ————	4	1	1
Mr. *Stevenson*'s Chef. M. ————	1	2	3
Mr. *Wood*'s Bay H. ————	2	3	2
Mr. *Lifter*'s Bay M. ————	5	4	4
Mr. *Gibson*'s Chef. M. ————	3	dif	
Mr. *Stoker*'s Grey G. ————	dif		
Mr. *Storey*'s Chef. G. ————	dif		

On the 15th *ditto*, on the same Course; a 20 *l.* Plate was run for; *wt.* 10 *ft.* one Guin. and a half Entr.

Entr. Stakes for the 2d beſt. This Prize was the
Preſent of *Tho. Walton* Eſq; High Sheriff for this
County of *Northumberland*; and won by

	1 H.	2 H.	3 H.
Mr. *Lampton*'s Grey H. —————	1	1	2
Mr. *Fenwick*'s Grey G. *Smock-Face*—	2	2	1
Mr. *Bowes*'s Grey M. —————	3	3	3

On the 16th *ditto*, on the ſame Courſe, a Gold
Cup of 40 *l*. Value was run for; *wt*. 12 *ſt*. 3 Guin.
Entr.

	1 H.	2 H.
Which Prize was won by		
Sir *William Middleton*'s Cheſ. H. *Scipio*	1	1
Mr. *Hope*'s Grey G. —————————	3	2
Mr. *Carr*'s Black H. ————————	2	diſ

MORPETH.

On the 26th Day of *July*, a 10 *l*. Plate was run
for at *Morpeth*, being only for ſuch as never won
10 *l*. 14 Hands, to carry 10 *ſt*. and to give or take,
if higher or lower: 1 Guin. Entr.

	1 H.	2 H.	3 H.
This Prize was won by			
Mr. *Wood*'s Bay H. *Thro'-the-Woods-Laddy* —————————	1	1	2
Mr. *Croft*'s Grey G. *Now-or-never*—	4	2	1
Mr. *Carr*'s Grey H. *Can-run-and-will-not*————	3	3	3
Mr. *Jackſon*'s Grey G. *Bold-Thirkeld*	2	diſ	
Mr. *Hepple*'s Bay G. *Highland-Laddy*	diſ		

On the ſame Courſe, the following Day, a 20 *l*.
Plate was run for; *wt*. 10 *ſt*. one Guin. and a half
Entr. and won by

2   Mr.

	1 H.	2 H.	3 H.
Mr. *Unthank*'s Chef. G. *Little-thought of*	4	1	1
Mr. *Cook*'s Grey H. *Quiet*	1	2	2
Mr. *Cowel*'s Chef. M. *Flower-of-May*	3	3	3
Mr. *Fenwick*'s Bay G. *Quiet-Cuddy*	2	4	4
Mr. *Clark*'s Grey M.	5	5	5
Mr. *Charlton*'s Bay M. *Creeping-Molly*	6	dr.	

On the 28th *ditto*, upon this Courfe, a Plate of 10 Guineas Value was run for, being a Prefent to the Town by the Right Hon. the Lord *Morpeth*, and Sir *Tho. Robinfon* Bart. and being for Galloways, 10 ft. the higheft give and take, 1 Guin. Entr. Stakes for the 2d beft.

	1 H.	2 H.
This Plate was won by Mr. *Armftrong*'s Bay M. *Baker*, 13 H. 2 I. ¾	1	1
Mr. *Crefwell*'s Grey M. *Frofty-Face*, 13 H. 3 I.	2	2

On the Day following, upon the fame Courfe, a 20 l. Plate for fix Year Olds was run for; *wt.* 10 ft. 2 Guin. Entr. and won by

	1 H.	2 H.	3 H.
Mr. *Bowes*'s Black H. *Buck*	1	3	1
Mr. *Wilfon*'s Chef. M. *Swallow*	3	1	3
Sir *John Swinburn*'s Grey M. *Sweet-Lips*	2	2	2

A 5th and laft Prize of this Meeting, was a Gold Cup of 40 l. Value; *wt.* 10 ft. 3 Guin. Entr. and won by

Mr.

	1 H.	2 H.
Mr. *Hudfon*'s Chef. H. *Fair-Play* ———	1	1
Sir *William Middleton*'s Chef. H. *Scipio*	2	2

Enter for the two firſt of theſe Prizes, on the 10th; for the other three, on the 2ad *ditto* : and four, if infiſted on, were each Day obliged to ſtart.

MILFIELD-GREEN.

On the 20th of *Augaſt*, at *Milfield-Green*, Mr. *Swinburn*'s Grey G. beat Mr. *Nelſon*'s Grey M. three ſeveral four Miles Heats; 10 *l*. 20 Guin. *per* Heat.

***

OXFORDSHIRE, 1731.

GORING-HEATH.

ON the 8th Day of *July*, a Purſe of 20 Guineas was run for at *Goring-Heath*, free only for ſuch as never won 20 *l*. 14 Hands, to carry 9 *ſt*. and to give or take, if higher or lower: the Winner to be ſold for 30 *l*. to ent. on the 1ſt *ditto*, paying 1 Guin. or two at the Poſt.

	1 H.	2 H.
This Prize was won by		
Mr. *Price*'s Bay M. *Stay-till-I-come* ———	1	1
Mr. *Clark*'s Brown H. *Fear-not* ———	2	2
Mr. *Waller*'s Mouſe-colour'd G. *Shadow*	6	3
Mr. *Gale*'s Bay G. ———	3	dr.
Mr. *Gore*'s Bay M. *Miſs-Pret* ———	4	dr.
Mr. *Garrard*'s Black G. *Othello* ———	5	dr.

K   On

On the following Day, upon this Courfe, a Purfe of 10 Guineas was run for, free only for fuch as never won 10 Guin. *wt.* 10 *ſt.* to ent. alfo on the 1ſt *ditto,* paying half a Guin. or one Guin. at the Poſt.

This Prize was won by	1 H.	2 H.	3 H.
Mr. *Clark*'s Brown H. *Black-Legs* ——	3	1	1
Sir *Hen. Inglefield*'s Grey H. ——	1	3	2
Mr. *Boot*'s Brown G. *Wat-Reding* ——	4	2	3
Mr. *Fugger*'s Sorrel G. *Why-not* ——	2	dr.	
Sir *Hen. Jennings*'s Black G——	dif		

City of OXFORD.

On the 31ſt Day of *Auguſt,* a Purfe of 50 Guin. was run for at *Oxford,* free for any that never won a Royal Plate; *wt.* 12 *ſt.* 3 Guin. Entr.

This Prize was won by	1 H.	2 H.	3 H.
Sir *Hump. Monoux*'s Dun G. *Fox-hunter* ——	3	1	1
Mr. *Tuting*'s Brown M. *Cynder-Wench* ——	1	2	2
Mr. *How*'s Brown H. *Penfioner* ——	2	3	3

On the 1ſt of *September,* on the fame Courfe, a Purfe of 10 Guineas was run for, free only for fuch Galloways as never won above 10 Guineas; 9 *ſt.* the higheſt give and take: half a Guin. Entr.

This Prize was won by	1 H.	2 H.
Mr. *Penruddock*'s Chef. M. *Mifs-Poppet,* 13 H. 2 I. ½ ——	1	1
Mr. *Holman*'s Grey G. *Tantivy,* 13 H. 2 I. ½ ——	3	2
Mr. *Holder*'s Chef. M. *Nut-Brown-Maid,* 13 H. 2 I. ——	2	3

On

On the 2d *ditto*, on the same Course, a Purse of 20 Guin. was run for, free only for such as never won above 40 Guin. *wt.* 10 *st.* 1 Guin. Entr.

	1 H.	2 H.
This Prize was won by		
Mr. *Thatcher*'s Bay M. *Fair-Rosamond* ——	1	1
Ld *Ranelagh*'s Bay M. *Fanny's-alone* ——	2	2

A 3d Prize of this Meeting, was a Purse of 30 Guin. free only for such six Year Olds as never won a King's Plate; *wt.* 10 *st.* and won by

	1 H.	2 H.
Mr. *How*'s Bay H. *King's-Fisher* ————	1	1
Mr. *Grisewood*'s Grey G. *Sharper* ——	2	2
Mr. *Garrard*'s Chess. H. *Dragoon* ———	3	dis

Enter for each Prize, respectively, 7 Days before Running.

🌼🌼🌼🌼🌼🌼🌼🌼🌼🌼🌼🌼🌼🌼🌼🌼🌼🌼🌼🌼

SHROPSHIRE, 1731.

SHREWSBURY.

ON the 16th Day of *June*, a free Purse of 40 Guineas was run for at *Shrewsbury*, *wt.* 11 *st.* 3 Guineas Entr. which Prize was won by

	1 H.	2 H.
Mr *Williams Wynn*'s Bay H. *Spot*——	1	1
Mr. *Williams*'s Black H. *Sloven* ——	3	2
Mr. *Puleston*'s Chess. H. *Surly* ——	2	dis
Mr. *Lechmere*'s Bay G. *Gulliver*, often call'd *Batt* ——	dis	

On

On the 17th *ditto*, upon this Course, the Lady's Subſcription (conſiſting of Ten Guineas) was run for, free only for Galloways, 9 ſt. the higheſt give and take, one Guinea Entr. and won by

	1 H.	2 H.
Mr. *Lee*'s Bay G. *Wanton-Willy*, 13 H. 3 I. ½ ———	1	1
Mr. *Coles*'s Cheſ. G. *Little-Eſquire*, 14 H. ———	2	2
Mr. *Atkis*'s Bay G. *Would-if-he-could*, 13 H. 2 I. ¾ ———	*diſ*	

The laſt Prize of this Meeting was a 20 Guin. Plate, on the following Day; free only for ſuch Hunters of the paſt Seaſon, as never ſtarted for the Value of 10 *l. wt.* 10 ſt. 2 Guineas Entr.

	1 H.	2 H.
This Prize was won by		
Mr. *Holland*'s Cheſ. M. *Creeping-Kate*	1	1
Mr. *Lechmere*'s Grey H. *Buck-hunter*———	2	2
Mr. *Taylor*'s Cheſ. G. *Now-Club-or-never*———	3	3

Enter for each Prize, reſpectively, 3 days before Running.

On the 12th of *October*, upon this Course, a Purſe of 10 Guineas was run for, *wt.* 10 ß, and won by

	1 H.	2 H.
Mr. *Sandford*'s Bay G. ———	1	
Mr. *Piggot*'s Dun G.———	*diſ*	
Mr. *Taylor*'s Cheſ. G. ———	*diſ*	
Mr. *Corbet*'s Grey M. ———	*diſ*	

OSWESTRY.

On the 22d of *July*, a Purse of 20 Guineas was run for at *Oswestry*, wt. 10 ft. 2 Guineas Entr. and won by

	2 H.
Mr. *Williams*'s Black H. *Sloven* ——	1
Mr. *Hurst*'s Bay G. *Wanton-Willy* ——	2

On the same Course, on the following Day, was 10 Guineas, for Galloways, 9 ft. the highest give and take, one Guinea Entr. and won by

	1 H.	2 H.
Mr. *Hill*'s Chef. M. *Lady-Legs*, 13 H. 2 I.	1	1
Mr. *Holland*'s Bay M. *Creeping-Kate* ——	3	2
Mr. *Hurst*'s Bay G. *Wanton-Willy*, 13 H. 3 I. ½ ——	2	dr.

A 3d and last Prize of this Meeting, was a free Purse of 30 Guineas, wt. 12 ft. 3 Guineas Entr. and won by

	1 H.
Mr. *Williams Wynn*'s Bay H. *Spot* ——	1
Mr. *Williams*'s Black H. *Sloven* ——	2

LUDLOW.

On the 30th of *August*, a Purse of 50 Guineas was run for, free only for such 6 Year Olds, as never won a Royal Plate, wt. 11 ft. to enter on the 23d *ditto*, paying 3 Guin. Stakes for the 2d best.

	1 H.	2 H.	3 H.
This Prize was won by			
Mr. *Herbert*'s Bay H. *Wanton-Willy*	1	4	1
Sir *Henry Inglefield*'s Grey H. *Why-not*	4	1	2
Mr. *Neal*'s Black H. *Sloven* ——	3	2	3

K 3   Mr.

	1 H.	2 H.	3 H.
Mr. *Price's* Chef. M. *Faultless*———	5	3	dif
Mr. *Cornewall's* Chef. H. *Prince-of-Wales* ———	2	dr.	

On the 31st *ditto*, upon this Course, was a 20*l.* Plate, for Hunters, *wt.* 11 *ß.* to enter on the 24th *ditto*, paying 2 Guineas.

	1 H.	2 H.
This Prize was won by		
Mr. *Onkly's* Grey G. *Merry-Dick*———	1	1
Mr. *Bruce's* Grey M. *Merry-Lass* ———	2	2
Mr. *Neale's* Bay M. *Frosty-Face* ———	3	dif
Mr. *Carrington's* Bay G. *Shapeless* ———	dif	

On the 1st Day of *September*, on the same Course, a free Plate of 30*l.* value was run for, *wt.* 10*ß.* to enter on the 25th of *July*, paying 2 Guineas Stakes for the 2d best.

	1 H.	2 H.	3 H.
This Prize was won by			
Mr. *Mackworth's* Grey H. *Fear-not*———	1	1	4
Sir *Richard Grosvenor's* Chef. H. *Terror*	4	3	1
Mr. *Musters's* Bay M. *Diana*———	2	4	2
Mr. *Neale's* Chef. M. *Peggy-grieves-me*	3	2	3
Sir *John Astley's* Chef. H. *Highland-Laddy* ———	dif		

MARKET-DREYTON.

On the 16th Day of *September*, a free Purse of 20 Guineas was run for at *Dreyton*, *wt.* 10*ß.* and won by

	1 H.	
Mr. *Masters's* Bay M. *Diana*———	1	
Mr. *Mackworth's* Bay H.———	dif	

The

The 10 Guineas, for Galloways, on the following Day, were not run for.

❧❧❧❧❧❧❧❧❧❧ ❧❧❧❧ ❧❧❧❧❧❧❧❧❧❧

SOMERSETSHIRE, 1731.

City of BATH.

ON the 26th Day of *May*, a Purse of 10 Guin. was run for at *Bath*, free for Galloways, 9 *ft*. the highest give and take, half a Guinea Entr. which Prize was won by

	H.
Mr. *Coles*'s Black G. *Little-Esquire* ———	1
Mr. *Baskervile*'s Grey M. *Smiling-Molly*	2
Mr. *Winnick*'s Black M. *Gipsy* ———	*dif*

On the Day following, upon this Course, a 20 Guinea Purse was run for, *wt*. 10 *ft*. Entr. one Guin. and won by

	H.
Mr. *Coles*'s Grey M. *Painted-Lady* ———	1
Mr. *Biggs*'s Black G. ———————	2

Enter for both the 22d *ditto*, and 3 each Day were obliged to start.

꧁꧂꧁꧂꧁꧂꧁꧂꧁꧂꧁꧂

STAFFORDSHIRE, 1731.

BURTON upon TRENT.

UPON this Courfe, on the 29th of *March*, Mr. *Oldershaw*'s Chef. M. beat Mr. *Campion*'s Roan M. 4 Miles, *wt.* a Feather, 10 Guin.

City of LITCHFIELD.

On the 21ft of *September*, a 20 *l.* Plate was run for at *Litchfield*, free only for fuch Hunters as never won 5 *l.* nor ftarted for 10; *wt.* 12 *ft.* 2 Guineas Entr. which Prize was won by

	1 H.	2 H.
Sir *William Wolfeley*'s Bay M. *Almahide*	1	1
Mr. *Littleton*'s Brown G. *Play-fellow*—	2	2
Mr. *Horton*'s Brown H. *Who-can-tell*—	3	3
Mr. *Salt*'s Brown G. *Jack-of-the-Green*	dif	

On the fame Courfe, the following Day, was 10 Guineas, for Galloways, 9 *ft.* the higheft give and take, 2 Guineas Entr. and won by

	1 H.
Mr. *Sidebottom*'s Chef. M. *Lady-Legs*, 13 H. 2 I. ¾———	1
Mr. *Allestry*'s Grey H. *Smiling-Tom*	2
Mr. *Pritchard*'s Bay G. *Now-or-never*, 13 H. 1 I. ———	3

On

On the 23d *ditto*, on the same Course, a 40*l.* Plate was run for, being free, and the *wt.* 12 *ft.* 3 Guineas Entr. which Prize was won by

	1 H.	2 H.	3 H.
Mr. *Williams Wynn*'s Bay H. *Spot* ———	3	1	1
Hon. Mr. *Gower*'s Grey H. *Jack-of-the-Green* ———	1	2	3
Duke of *Ancaster*'s Grey H. *Gentleman* ———	2	3	2

Enter for all three on the 20th *ditto*.

Town of STAFFORD.

On the 29th of *September*, a free Plate of 20 *l.* value, was run for at *Stafford*, *wt.* 10 *ft.* 2 Guin. Entr. and won by

	1 H.	2 H.
Mr. *Burton*'s Bay M. *Moor-Poote* ———	1	1
Mr. *Mußers*'s Bay M. *Diana* ———	2	2
Sir *William Wolseley*'s Bay M. *Almahide* ———	dif	
Mr. *Mackworth*'s Bay H. *Stand-by-Clear-the-Way*. He took the Rest, and was ———	dif	

On the same Course, on the following Day, was a 10 *l.* Plate, for Galloways, 9 *ft.* the highest give and take; for which there started Mr. *Sidebottom*'s Chef. M. *Lady-Legs*, and Mr. *Rhodes*'s Chef. G. *Merry-Barnaby*; but the latter starting only to qualify the other, and taking up immediately, retiring back to his Stable; the Company took Offence at it, and prevented the Mare from running the Heat through, and thereupon refus'd to deliver her the Plate.

New-

NEWCASTLE under LINE.

On the 7th Day of *October*, a free Plate of 20 *l.* value, was run for at *Newcastle*, *wt.* 10 *st.* and the Winner to be fold for 40 *l.* which Prize was won by

	1 H.	2 H.
Mr. *Barton*'s Bay M. *Moore-Poote* ———	1	1
Mr. *Kirby*'s Bay M. *Statira* ———	2	2
Mr. *Oldham*'s Grey H. *Run-now-or-hunt-for-ever* ———	3	dr.

On the fame Courfe, on the following Day, a 10 Guineas Prize was run for, 14 Hands, to carry 10 *st.* and to give or take, if higher or lower; which Prize was alfo won by

	1 H.	2 H.
Mr. *Barton*'s Bay M. *Moore-Poote*, 14 H. ¾	1	1
Mr. *Sidebottom*'s Chef. M. *Lady-Legs*, 13 H. 2 I. ½ ———	2	2

A 3d and laft Prize of this Meeting was 15 Guin. for Hunters, on the following Day, *wt.* 10 *st.*

For which Mr. *Langley*'s Bay M. *Pleafant-Betty*, ftarted alone; but the Articles requiring two at leaft to ftart, I hear the Prize was refus'd her.

SURREY, 1731.

EPSOM.

IN the Beginning of *April* at *Epfom*, Mr. *Grant*'s Bay M. beat Mr. *Ryley*'s Grey G. 12 *st.* 5 ℔. 4 Miles, 20 Guineas.

On

On the 11th of *May*, upon this Course, a Purse of 40 Guineas was run for, free only for such six Year Olds, as never won a King's Plate, *wt.* 10 * st.* and won by

	1 H.	2 H.
Mr. *Nevlin*'s Bay H. *Huffar* ——————	1	1
Mr. *Colvin*'s Bay H. *Fox-hunter* ——————	5	2
Mr. *Jenison*'s Bay H. *Magpye* —————	2	4
Mr. *Shuttleworth*'s Dun M. *Molly* —————		
Rev. Mr. *Gwyn*'s Chef. H. *Merry-man*		
Mr. *Major*'s Grey G. *White-Stockings* —		

On the following Day, upon this Course, was 20 Guineas, for Galloways, 9 *st.* the highest give and take, and won by

	1 H.	2 H.
Mr. *Trewet*'s Grey H. 13 H. 2 I. ¾ —————	1	1
Ld *Hamilton*'s Grey M. *Northern-Nancy*, 13 H. 2 I. ½ ————— }	3	[2
Mr. *Pierce*'s Grey H. *Harmless*, 14 H. —	2	3

On the 13th *ditto*, upon this Course, a Purse of 30 Guineas was run for, free for any that never won above 50 Guin. *wt.* 10 *st.* and won by

	1 H.	2 H.
Mr. *Trewet*'s Brown H. ————— —————	1	1
Mr. *Ireland*'s Chef. M. *Venus* ——————	3	2
Mr. *Shirly*'s Chef. G. *Smiling-Tom* ——	2	3
Mr. *Harvey*'s Bay H. *Fidler* ——————	4	4
Mr. *Cradock*'s Chef. M. *Now-or-never*—	5	dr.
Sir *Thomas Austin*'s Grey H. *Dufty-Miller* ————— }	dif	
Sir *Arthur Haflerige*'s Chef. H. *Who-can-tell* ————— }	dif	

A 4th Prize of this Meeting was a Purfe of 20 Guineas, on the following Day, free only for fuch as never won above 20 Guineas, *wt.* 12 *ft.* and won by

	1 H.	2 H.
Mr. *Cooper*'s Black H. *Scare-crow* ———	1	1
Mr. *Clark*'s Grey H. *Stradler* ———	3	2
Mr. *Armftrong*'s Grey H, *Cripple* ———	2	dr.

A 5th and laft Prize of this Meeting, was a 30 Guineas Purfe, on the 15th *ditto*, free only for 5 Year Olds, *wt.* 9 *ft.* 2 Miles at a Heat.

	1 H.	2 H.	3 H.
This Prize was won by			
Mr. *Elftob*'s Brown H. *Monkey* ———	5	1	1
Mr. *Gooftry*'s Grey H. *Wanton-Willy*	1	2	2
Hon. Mr. *Greville*'s Bay G. *Brimmer*	2	3	3
Mr. *Ireland*'s Sorrel M. *Shadow* ———	3	4	dr.
Mr. *Turner*'s Dun G. ———	4	5	dr.
Mr. *Colvin*'s Bay M. *Poor-Moll* ———	6	dr.	

The Entrance-Money for thefe Prizes was as follows;

For the 1ft Prize 4 Guin. or 6 at the Poft.

For the 2d, 2 Guin. or 4 at the Poft.

For the 3d, 3 Guin. or 5 at the Poft.

For the 4th, 2 Guin. or 4 at the Poft.

And for the 5th and laft Prize, 3 Guin. or 5 at the Poft: And three each Day were oblig'd to ftart.

On the 22d *ditto*, upon this Courfe, Mr. *Pellet*'s Chef. H. beat Mr. *Hamly*'s Bay M. 12 *ft.* 4 Miles, 20 Guineas.

Upon this Courfe, on the 7th Day of *September*, a Purfe of 40 Guineas was run for, free for any that never won a King's Plate, *wt.* 11 *ft.* and won by

Mr.

	1 H.	2 H.	3 H.
Mr. *Tuting's* Brown M. *Cinder-Wench*	3	1	1
Mr. *Glanvill's* Chef. H. *Smiling-Ball*	2	2	2
Mr. *Green's* Chef. H. *Merry-Andrew*	1	dif	

On the following Day, upon the fame Courfe, a 20 Guinea Purfe was run for, free only for fuch Galloways, as never won above 50 Guineas, 9 ft. the higheft give and take, and won by Mr. *Griffin*, with a Hack that he ftarted to make the Number of three.

On the following Day, a Purfe of 30 Guineas was run for, on the fame Courfe, free for any that never won above 50 Guineas, *wt.* 10 ft. and won by

	1 H.	2 H.
Mr. *Griffin's* Grey H. *Smugler*———	1	1
Mr. *Fagg's* Grey H. *Cripple* ———	3	2
Mr. *Ireland's* Chef. M. *Venus*———	2	3
Mr. *Harris's* Bay H. *Sobriety* ———	dif	

The Entrance-Money for thefe three Prizes was,
For the 1ft 4 Guin. or 6 at the Poft.
For the 2d 2 Guin. or 4 at the Poft.
And for the 3d 3 Guin. or 5 at the Poft.

And three again were oblig'd each Day to ftart.

I have obferv'd before, that 'tis a ftanding Rule at this Place, to enter at the Poft for each Prize, or 14 Days before the 1ft Day of the Meeting.

They are alfo, come to a Refolution, to have fix Prizes in the fucceeding Spring; 3 of them to be run for in the 1ft Week in *May*, and 3 in the 2d.

L   LYMPS-

LYMPSFIELD.

On the 26th Day of *July*, a 15 *l*. Plate was run for at *Lympsfield*, free only for such as never won a Plate of that Value, *wt.* 10 *st.* and won by

	1 H.	2 H.
Mr. *Clark*'s Brown H. *Fear-not* ———	1	1
Mr. *Fleetwood*'s Grey G. ———	4	2
Mr. *Smith*'s Bay M. ———	3	3
Mr. *Plumley*'s Bay G. ———	2	dif

On the 27th *ditto*, on the same Course, was a 10 *l*. Plate for Galloways, 8 *st.* the highest give and take, and won by

	1 H.	2 H.
Mr. *Hardy*'s Grey M. *Sweet-tem-per'd-Lady*, 14 H. ———	1	1
Mr. *Moss*'s Grey G. 13 H. 3 I. ———	2	2

WIMBLETON.

On the 10th Day of *August*, a Purse of 10 Guin. was run for at *Wimbleton*, 14 Hands, to carry 9 *st.* and to give or take, if higher or lower.

This Prize was won by	1 H.	2 H.	3 H.
Mr. *Griffin*'s Grey M. *Creeping-Kate*, 14 H. 1 I. $\frac{1}{4}$ $\frac{1}{2}$ q. ———	3	2	1
Mr. *Bonas*'s Bay H. *Squirrel*, 13 H. 3 I. $\frac{1}{4}$ ———	2	3	dif
Mr. *Trimmer*'s Chef. H. *Favourite*, lam'd and drawn, 13 H. 2 I. —	3	dr.	dr.
Mr. *Ratcatcher*'s Bay M. 13 H. $\frac{1}{2}$ I. —	4	dr.	
Mr. *Lawrance*'s Black G. *Stay-till-I-come*, 13 H. 3 I. $\frac{1}{4}$ ———	5	dr.	

Mr.

	1 H.		
Mr. *Hardy*'s Grey M. *Sweet-tem-* *per'd-Lady,* 13 H. 3 I. ¼ —— }	dif		

On the 28th Day of *September*, on the same Course, a 2d Purse of 10 Guin. was run for, *wt.* also the same, and won by

	1 H.	2 H.	3 H.
Ld *Hamilton*'s Grey M. *Northern-* *Nancy,* 13 H. 2 I. —— }	2	1	1
Mr. *Penruddock*'s Chef. M. *Miss-* *Poppet,* 13 H. 2 I. ¼ —— }	1	2	2
A Hack to qualify ——	dif		

SUFFOLK, 1731.

BECCLES.

ON the 25th Day of *June*, a 10 *l.* Purse was run for at *Beccles,* being for Galloways, 9 *ft.* the highest give and take, and won by

	1 H.	2 H.
The Revd. Mr. *Burnet*'s Grey H. *Thiller* —— }	1	1
Mr. *South*'s Brown H. *Brown-Darcy*	2	2
Mr. *Tasburg*'s Brown H. fell ——	dif	
Mr. *Johnson*'s Bay H. ——	dif	
Mr. *Smith*'s Bay M. ——	dif	

On the following Day, on the same Course, a 30 Guineas Purse was run for, *wt.* 10 *ft.* and won by

	1 H.	2 H.	3 H.
Mr. *Robe*'s Chef. M. *Sweetest-when-naked*	1	1	3
Mr. *Tuting*'s Bay H. *Squirrel*	3	3	1
Mr. *South*'s Grey M.	2	2	2
Mr. *Cooke*'s Bay M.			
Mr. *Hayes*'s Chef. H.			

BUNGEY.

On the 23d Day of *August*, a Purse of 10 Guin. was run for at *Bungey*, free for Galloways, 9 *st.* the highest give and take, and won by

	1 H.	2 H.
Mr. *Webster*'s Grey M. *Jilting-Jenny*, 13 H. 3 I. $\frac{1}{2}$	1	1
Mr. *Catton*'s Grey G. *Dobbin*, 13 H. 3 I. $\frac{1}{2}$	2	2
Mr. *Johnson*'s Brown H. *Stay-till-I-come*, 13 H. 3 I.	4	3
Mr. *Tasburg*'s Brown H. *Mute*, 13 H. 3 I. $\frac{1}{2}$	3	4

On the following Day, on the fame Courfe, a Purfe of 20 *l.* Sterling was run for, free for any that never won 30 *l. wt.* 10 *st.* which Prize was alfo won by

	1 H.	2 H.	3 H.
Mr. *Webster*'s *Jilting-Peggy*	1	1	3
Mr. *Tasburg*'s Grey H. *Thin-Breeches*	5	2	1
Mr. *Cleever*'s White G. *Poker*	2	3	2
Mr. *Catton*'s Grey G. *Dobbin*	4	4	dr.
Mr. *Botright*'s Bay G. *Fortune*	3	5	dr.
Mr. *Kettle*'s Chef. G. *Labour-in-vain*	6	dr.	

SUSSEX, 1731.

ARUNDEL.

ON the 11th of *May*, a Purse of 20 Guineas was run for at *Arundel*, 14 Hands, to carry 10 *st.* and to give or take, if higher or lower.

	1 H.	2 H.
Which Prize was won by		
Mr. *Orm*'s Chef. G. *Nicholina*, 14 H. $\frac{1}{2}$ I.	1	1
Mr. *Spence*'s Bay M. *Thoughtless*, 14 H. 2 I. $\frac{1}{4}$	4	2
Mr. *Fugger*'s Sorrel G. *Gimcrack*, 14 H.	2	3
Mr. *Vaughan*'s Bay M. *Judy*, 13 H. 3 I. $\frac{1}{4}$	3	4
Mr. *Curtis*'s Bay H. *Doctor*, 14 H.	dis	

MIDHURST.

On the *Thursday* in *Whitsun-Week*, the accustom'd Present of His Grace the Duke of *Somerset*, was run for at *Midhurst*, consisting of a Plate of 16 *l.* Value, *wt.* 10 *st.* and won by

	1 H.	2 H.
Mr. *Gruggin*'s Bay H. *Crutches*	1	1
Mr. *Vaughan*'s Bay M. *Judy*	2	2
Mr. *Pruit*'s Grey G. *Bonny-George*	3	3

City of CHICHESTER.

On the 17th of *June*, a Purse of 20 Guineas was run for at *Chichester*, free only for such as never

won

won 15 Guineas; 14 Hands, to carry 9 *st.* and to give or take, if higher or lower: to ent. on the 14th *ditto*, paying 2 Guin. or 4 at the Post.

Which Prize was won by	1 H.	2 H.	3 H.
Mr. *Vaughan*'s Grey M. *Have-it-if-she-can* ———	3	1	1
Mr. *Gruggin*'s Bay G. *Skeleton*———	2	2	2
Mr. *Heberden*'s Grey M. *Smiling-Molly*———	1	dis	

EAST-BOURN.

On the 9th Day of *Septemb.* a 10 *l.* Plate was run for at *East-Bourn*; *wt.* 10 *st.* and won by

	1 H.	2 H.
Mr. *Lidgiter*'s Black G. *Chimney-Sweeper*	2	1
Mr. *Selby*'s Brown H. *Swallow*———	1	dr.
Mr. *Vincent*'s Grey M. *Ace-of-Hearts*—	dis	
Mr. *Vaughan*'s Bay M. *Judy*———	dis	
Mr. *Bayley*'s Bay M. *Silver-Tail* ———	dis	

On the 10th *ditto*, on the same Course, a 25 *l.* Purse was run for; *wt.* also 10 *st.* and won by

	1 H.	2 H.
Mr. *Clark*'s Brown H. *Fear-not*———	1	1
Sir *Walter Parker*'s Bay M. *Silver-Tail*—	3	2
Mr. *Spence*'s Bay M. *Thoughtless* ———	2	dis

WEST-

WESTMORELAND, 1731.

KERBY-LONSDALE.

ON the 29th of *April*, on this Course, the following four started for a Plate of 10*l.* Value, and 10 Guin. Cash; *wt*. 10*ft.*

	1 H.	2 H.	3 H.
The same was won by			
Mr. *Smith*'s Bay M. *Touch-and-take*	3	1	1
Mr. *Thornton*'s Grey G. *Creeper* ————	1	2	2
Mr. *Salkield*'s Bay M. *Camilla* ———	4	dif	
Mr. *Jennison*'s Bay M. *Faustina* ————	2	dr.	

APPLEBY.

On the 13th Day of *May*, a 10*l.* Plate was run for at *Appleby*; *wt*. 10*ft.* and won by

	1 H.	2 H.
Mr. *Parkins*'s Brown M. *Muslin-Face* —	2	1
Mr. *Greathead*'s Grey G. ————————	1	2
Mr. *Salkield*'s Chef. M. *Camilla* ————	3	3

WILT-

WILTSHIRE, 1731.

MARLBOROUGH.

ON the 11th Day of *August*, a Purse of 50 Guineas was run for at *Marlborough*, free only for such as never won a King's Plate; *wt.* 10*st.* Ent. 3 Guin. or 5 at the Post, Stakes 17 Guin.

Which Prize was won by	1 H.	2 H.	3 H.	4 H.
Mr. *Tuting's* Brown M. *Cynder-Wench*	4	1	2	1
Hon. Mr. *Bertie's* Chef. M. *Lady-Thigh*	5	3	1	2
Mr. *Sheppard's* Bay G. *Bold-Thirkeld*	1	2	3	3
Mr. *Hetherd's* Grey H. *Grey-Hobler*	2	dr.		
Mr. *Long's* Bay G. *Caft-away*	3	dr.		

On the following Day, on this Course, a Purse of 20 Guineas was run for, free for any that never won 20 Guin. *wt.* 12*st.* and the Winner to be sold for 30 Guin. Stakes 7 Guin.

This Prize was won by	1 H.	2 H.	3 H.
Mr. *Tuting's* Grey M. *Scotchman's-Pack-Carrier*	2	1	1
Mr. *Cawley's* Brown G. *Smiling-Tom*	1	2	3
Mr. *Figg's* Grey M. *Unfortunate-Lady*	3	3	2
Mr. *Barnes's* Chef. H. *Merry-Andrew*	4	dif	

On

On the 13th *ditto*, on he same Course, a 20*l.* Plate, was run for, being a present to the Town, by the Right Hon. the Lord ʳᵘᶜᵉ, and free for Galloways; 9 *ft.* the higheſt giv and take, Stakes 5 Guin.

	1 H.	2 H.	3 H.
This Prize was won by			
Sir *Arthur Haſlerige*'s Bay M. *Ring-Tail*, 13 H. 2 I. ¼	2	1	
Mr. *Sheppard*'s Bay M. *Whimſy*, 13 H. 3 I. ¼	1	2	2
Sir *John Dutton*'s Brown H. *Start-away*, 13 H. 3 I. ½	3	3	3
Mr. *Canby*'s Cheſ. M. *Rattle*, 13 H. 1 I.	diſ		
Mr. *Nalder*'s Brown G. *Brownwood*, 14 H.	diſ		

The 2d beſt in each of theſe three Days, was intitled to the Stakes, even if diſtanc'd; which Method will be continued. The Prizes also at this Place will continue the ſame; but the Weight alter'd from 12 *ft.* to 11. They'll also be run for at the ſame time of the Year.

WORCESTERSHIRE, 1731.

LONGMORE-HEATH.

ON the 14th of *June*, upon *Longmore-Heath*, Mr. *Hurſt*'s Grey H. *Spot*, beat Mr. *Kirby*'s Bay G. *Nicholina*, 12 *ft.* 6 *m.* 50 Guin. The Gelding gave a Diſtance at ſtarting.

WAR-

WARWICKSHIRE, 1731.

STRATFORD UPON AVON.

ON the 22d of *July*, a 30 *l*. free Plate was run for at *Stratford*, wt. 11 *st.* 3 Gain. Entr. and won by

	1st H.	2d H.
Mr. *Coke's* Bay M. *Statira* ———————	1	1
Mr. *Lechmere's* Bay G. *Baf* ————————	3	2
Mr. *Green's* Chef. H. *Handfome-Bob* ——	2	3
Mr. *Bray's* Chef. H. ——————————	4	dr.

On the fame Courfe, on the following Day, a 20 *l*. Plate was run for, *wt.* 10 *st.* and the Winner to be fold for 30 Guin. 2 Guin. Entr.

	1st H.	2d H.
This Prize was won by		
Mr. *Thatcher's* Bay M. *Fair-Rofamond* ·	1	1
Mr. *Woodman's* Grey H. *Sly* —————	3	2
Mr. *Dawkins's* Chef. H. ———————	4	3
Mr. *Coles's* Grey M. *Painted-Lady* ———	2	4
Mr. *Holman's* Grey H. ———————	dif	

Town of WARWICK.

On the 25th Day of *August*, a 50 *l*. Gold Cup was run for at *Warwick*; wt. 12 *st.* to ent. *Saturday* before, paying 4 Guin.

	1st H.	2d H.
This Prize was won by		
Mr. *Coke's* Chef. H. *Tarran* —————	1	1
Mr. *Williams-Wynn's* Bay H. *Spot* ———	2	2

On

On the same Course, on the following Day, was a 10l. Plate for Galloways; for which Mr. *Coles's* *Little-Esquire* started alone.

On the 27th *ditto*, a 20l. Plate was run for on this Course; *wt.* 10 *st.* the Winner to be sold for 30 Guineas: to ent. 7 Days before, paying 2 Guin.

	1 H.	2 H.	3 H.
This Prize was won by			
Mr. *Thatcher's* Bay M. *Fair-Rosamond*	3	1	1
Mr. *Woodman's* Grey G. *Sly* ————	1	2	2
Mr. *Bradly's* Bay H. *Patch* ————	2	3	dr.

ATHERSTONE.

On the 15th of *Septemb.* the following Galloways started for a 10 l. Plate at *Atherstone*; 9 st. the highest give and take.

	1 H.	2 H.
Mr. *Fleetwood's* Chef. H. *Lilliput* ————	1	1
Mr. *Henly's* Bay H. *Pebble-Stone* ————	2	2
A Back to Qualify ————————	dif	

On the 16th *ditto*, on the same Course, a 20l. Plate was run for, *wt.* 10 *st.* and won by

	1 H.	2 H.	3 H.
Mr. *Coles's* Grey M. *Painted-Lady* —	2	1	1
Mr. *Froggat's* Grey M. *Derbyshire-Sally* ————	1	2	2

BITFORD.

On the 1st Day of *Octob.* a Purse of 10l. *Sterl.* was run for at *Bitford*; *wt.* 10 *st.* and won by

	1 H.	2 H.
Mr. *Plampin's* Grey G. *King's-Fisher* —	1	1
Mr. *Hewet's* Grey H. *Brown-Tavern* ———	3	2
Mr. *Kirby's* Bay G. *Nicholina* ————	2	3
Mr. *Kendrick's* Bay M. *Coscomb-Polly* —	4	dif
Mr. *Herbert's* Grey H. ————	dif	
Capt. *Barnsby's* Chef. H. ————	dif	

YORK-

YORKSHIRE, 1731.

KIPLING-COATS.

ON the 3d *Thursday* in *March*, as usual, the 16 Guineas were run for at *Kipling-Coats ;* *wt.* 10 *st.* one Heat, and won by

	1 H.
Mr. *Brewster*'s Bay M. *Miss-Nesham* ——	1
Mr. *Taylor*'s Bay M. *Polly-Peachum* ——	2

On the same Day, and Course, Mr. *Carvil*'s Grey H. beat Mr. *Bell*'s Bay H. 12 *st.* 4 Miles ; Mr. *Carvil* betting 120 Guineas to 80 Guin.

BOROUGH-BRIDGE.

In this Month of *March*, at *Borough-Bridge*, the following five Year Olds started for a Purse of 10 Guineas ; *wt.* 10 *st.*

	1 H.	2 H.	3 H.
Mr. *Mountain*'s Grey H *Fear-not* ——	3	1	1
Mr. *Clarke*'s Bay H. ——————	2	3	2
Sir *Reginald Greham*'s Bay M. ——	4	4	3
Mr. *Johnson*'s Chef. G. —————	1	2	dr.
Mr. *Loop*'s Grey M.——————	dif		

On the following Day, upon this Course, was 10 Guineas for Hunters ; *wt.* 10 *st.* and won by

2

Mr.

	1 H.	2 H.
Mr. *Tankred*'s Bay G. ————	1	1
Mr. *Read*'s Sorrel G. ————	2	2
Mr. *Yates*'s Bay M. ————	4	3
Mr. *Redſhaw*'s Bay G. ————	3	4

NEW-MALTON.

Upon this Courſe, on the 25th Day of *March*, Mr. *Cooper*'s Cheſ. M. *Sally-Salisbury*, 6 Years old, beat Mr. *Wrangham*'s Grey M. *Careleſs*, 5 Years old; 4 Miles, 10ſt. 20 Guin.

On the ſame Day, and Courſe, Mr. *Sympſon*'s Cheſ. G. *Smock-Face*, 4 Years old, 11ſt. 12℔. beat Mr. *Hood*'s Bay M. 5 Years old; 10ſt. 4 Miles, 20 Guin.

On the ſame Courſe, on the 29th Day of *June*, a 20*l*. Purſe was run for, free only for five Year Olds, *wt*. 9ſt. one Heat.

	1 H.	
This Prize was won by		
Mr. *Rokesby*'s Grey H. *Cobby* ————	1	
Mr. *Bartlet*'s Cheſ. H. *Bald-Snake* ———	2	
Mr. *Elſtob*'s Brown H. *Monkey* ———	3	
Mr. *Deighton*'s Grey M. the *Groom's-daily-Miſery* ——— ——— }	4	
Capt. *Gee*'s Brown H. *Fox-Cub* ———	5	
Mr. *Wrangham*'s Grey M. *Careleſs* ———	6	
Capt. *Appleyard*'s Bay M. *Caſt-away* ———	7	
Mr. *Whitfield*'s Grey H. *Who-can-tell* ———	8	
Mr. *Baldock*'s Bay M. *Miſs-Talbot* ———	9	

30th *ditto*, on the ſame Courſe, was 10*l*. for Galloways, 9ſt. the higheſt give and take; and won by

	1 H.	2 H.	3 H.
Mr. *Munday*'s Grey H. *Farmer*, 14 H.	1	1	2
Mr. *Lewin*'s Bay M. *Sweeteſt-when-naked*, 13 H. 2 I. ¼ ———— }	2	3	1

M   Mr.

	1 H.	2 H.	3 H.
Mr. *Barker's* Bay M. *Creeping-Kate*, 13 H. 1 I. ¾	3	2	dr.

The 30 Guineas advertised for the following Day at this Place, were not run for; but on that Day 10 *l. Sterl.* on the same Course, was run for; *wt.* 10 *ß.* and won by

	1 H.	2 H.
Mr. *Mountain's* Grey H. *Have-at-all*——	1	1
Mr. *Cooper's* Chef. M. *Sally-Salisbury*——	2	dr.

COOLHAM-DALE.

Upon this Course of *Coolham-Dale*, on the 25th of *March*, Mr. *Banton's* Grey H. got by *Smiling-Tom*, beat Mr. *Wright's* Bay M. both 5 Year Olds, 4 Miles, 10 *ß.* 20 Guin.

Upon this Course, on the 20th of *May*, Capt. *Appleyard's* Bay M. *Cast-away*, beat Mr. *Whitehead's* Grey H. *Who-can-tell*, 4 Miles, 10 *ß.* 100 Guin.

RICHMOND.

On the 4th of *May*, upon this Course, Mr. *Redshaw's* Bay G. 10 *ß.* beat Mr. *Robinson's* Grey M. 9 *ß.* 7 ℔. ½, 4 Miles, 20 Guin.

The three Prizes advertised for the present Year at this Place, were neither of them run for.

HUNMANBY.

Upon the 6th Day of *May*, a 20 *l.* Plate was run for at *Hunmanby*, free only for four Year Olds; *wt.* 9 *ß.* 1 Heat, Stakes for the 2d best.

There started for the same the five following.

Mr.

	H.
Mr. *Cowling*'s Chef. M. *White-Nofe*, full Sifter to *Peggy-grieves-me*, fhe won the s^d Heat and Plate———	1
Mr. *Thompfon*'s Bay M. *Mifs-Fox*, got by *Fox* ———	2
Mr. *Boyes*'s Bay H. *Careful*, got by Mr. *Bell*'s Horfe———	3
Mr. *Haffel*'s Bay H. *Cripple*, got by young *Childers*———	4
Mr. *Pockley*'s Black H. *Cripple*, was out of the crop'd Mare of the late Sir *Rich. Osbaldifton*'s, and got by *Champion* ———	5

MIDLAM.

On the 18th Day of *May*, at *Midlam*, Mr. *Bartlet*'s Bay M. beat Mr. *Benfon*'s Bay M. 9 ft. 4 Miles, 100 *l. Sterl.*

On the 22d of *Novemb.* upon this Courfe, Mr. *Furbank*'s Grey G. beat Mr. *Pindel*'s Bay M. 9 ft. 4 Miles, 10 Guin.

Upon this Courfe, on the 25th of *March* 1732. the Hon. Mr. *Vane*'s Grey Horfe *Midge*, ftands match'd to run againft Mr. *Hudfon*'s Chef. Horfe *Fair-Play*; 3 Heats, 9 ft. 50 Guineas a Heat.

KNARESBOROUGH.

On the 20th Day of *May*, a 15 Guin. Purfe was run for at *Knaresborough*, free only for 6 Year Olds; *wt.* 10 ft. 1 Guin. and half Entr. 3 Guin. as Stakes for the 2d beft.

	H.	H.
This Prize was won by	1	2
Mr. *Mountain*'s Grey H. *Fear-not*———	1	1
Mr. *Frankland*'s Bay M. *Pretty-Betty* —	2	2
Mr. *Cooper*'s Chef. M. *Sally-Salisbury* —	3	3

On

On the 21st *ditto*, upon this Course, was 10 Guin. for Galloways; 9 *st.* the highest give and take: 2 Guin. for the 2d best.

This Prize was won by	1 H.	2 H.
Mr. *Baines's* Grey H. *Spot*, 13 H. 3 I. ½	1	1
Mr. *Thompson's* Chef. M. *Little-Bitch*, 13 H. 3 I. ½	2	2
Mr. *Hedly's* Bay M. *Bouncing-Nell*	3	dr.

DONCASTER.

On the 2d Day of *June*, a Purse of 40 Guineas was run for at *Doncaster*, being for 6 Year Olds; *wt.* 12 *st.* 3 Guin. Entr.

This Prize was won by	1 H.	2 H.	3 H.
Mr. *Rickaby's* Black M. *Patch-Buttocks*	1	3	1
Mr. *Benson's* Bay H. *Lady's-Delight*	4	1	2
Mr. *Vavasor's* Chef. H. *Mercury*	2	2	3
Mr. *Bennet's* Bay G. *Star*	3	4	4

On the 3d *ditto*, on the same Course, a Purse of 15 Guin. was run for; *wt.* 10 *st.* and won by

	1 H.	2 H.	3 H.
Mr. *Wardle's* Bay M. *Miss-Betty*	1	1	
Mr. *Raven's* Grey G. *Little-worth*	3	4	1
Mr. *Hamnersley's* Bay G. *Bumper*	4	3	2
Mr. *Ridgway's* Bay H. *Little-John*	2	2	dif

In this 3d Heat, *Little-John* came in first, but was charged with foul Play, and for that reason was deem'd distanc'd, and the Heat and Stakes given to *Little-worth*.

The last Prize of this Meeting, was a 10 Guineas Purse for Galloways, 9 *st.* the highest give and take; half a Guin. Entr. This

	1 H.	2 H.
This Prize was won by		
Mr. *Whittle*'s Bay M. *Country-Wench,*		
13 H. 3 I. ½ ——————	1	1
Mr. *Morley*'s Bay G. 13 H. 2 I.————	2	2
Mr. *Walker*'s Grey M. *Diana*, 13 H. 2 I. ¼	*dis*	

Had but one, or two, enter'd for the 40 Guineas
at this Place, he or they were to receive 5 Guineas
each, and the Prize not run for.   The Stakes each Day
were for the 2d best, and 3 each Day were obliged
to start.   For this reason, the 20 Guin. advertised
for the 2d Day at this Place, were not run for;
but by agreement, the 15 Guin. as above.

'Tis a Resolution taken at this Place, that their
Plates for the future shall always be run for in the
first Week in *June*.

BEVERLY.

On the 8th Day of *June*, a free Purse of 25 Guin.
was run for at *Beverly*; *wt.* 10 *st.* 2 Guin. Entr.

This Prize was won by
Mr. *Heneage*'s Bay H. *White-Nose,* beating
Mr. *Thorold*'s Chef. M. *Diana.*
Mr. *Bourdenand*'s Bay M. *Polly-Peachum,* and
Mr. *Witty*'s Bay M. *Milk-Maid.*

On the same Course, the following Day, was 10
Guin. for Galloways; 9 *st.* the highest give and take,
1 Guin. Entr. and won by

	1 H.	2 H.
Mr. *Hedly*'s Bay M. *Bouncing-Nell* ———	1	1
Mr. *Thompson*'s Chef. M. *Little-Bitch*—	2	2
Mr. *Walbank*'s Grizled M. *Lady-Mil-singtown* —————		

On the 10th *ditto*, upon this Course, a 20 Guin. Purse was run for, being free for 5 Year Olds, only carrying 9 *st*. 3 Miles at a Heat, two Guineas Entr.

This Prize was won by	1 H.	2 H.	3 H.
Mr. *Thompson*'s Bay H. *Careless* ———		1	1
Mr. *North*'s Chef. H. *Gander* ———	1	2	5
Mr. *Hewson*'s Chef. H. *Careful*———			
Mr. *Binnington*'s Grey H. *Grey-Ramsden*——— }			
Mr. *Hutton*'s Brown M. *Tripping-Nancy* ——— }			

On the same Course, on the 11th *ditto*, was a 20 Guineas Purse, for 4 Year Olds, *wt.* 9 *st.* one Heat, two Guin. Entr.

This Prize was won by	1 H.
Mr. *Fawcit*'s Bay H. *Volpone*, got by *Fox* ——— }	1
Mr. *Sanderson*'s Grey M. *Sweet-Maidenhead*——— }	
Mr. *Wight*'s Brown H. *Thunderbolt*	
Mr. *Wilkinson*'s Grey M. *Chance* ———	
Mr. *Wyley*'s Bay M. *Smiling-Betty*———	
Mr. *Smith*'s Brown M. *Grievous*———	
Mr. *Hardesty*'s Chef. H. *Little-Durham*	

In each of these four Days the Stakes went to the 2d best; the Entr. Day was the 4th *ult.* and 3 each Day were oblig'd to start.

LAYBURN.

In the Month of *June*, a Purse of 15 Guin. was run for at *Layburn*, free only for 4 Year Olds, *wt.* 8 *st.* 7 *lb.* one 3 Miles Heat.

This

This Prize was won by

	1 H.
Mr. *Dalton*'s Grey H. ————————————	1
Duke of *Bolton*'s Grey H. He fell, or } had won———————————	2
Mr. *Chambers*'s Black M. She alſo fell	3

SELBEY.

On the 22d of *June*, a Purſe of 10 Guineas was run for at *Selbey, wt.* 10 *ſt.* and won by

	1 H.	2 H.
Mr. *Barton*'s Bay M. *Moore-Poote* ———	1	1
Mr. *Hedley*'s Bay M. *Bouncing-Nell* ———	2	2
Mr. *Palmes*'s Bay·M. ———————	3	3

BARNSLY.

On the 30th of *July*, a Purſe of 10 Guin. was run for at *Barnſly*, being for Galloways, 9 *ſt.* the higheſt give and take; and won by Mr. *Renders*'s. Bay M. *Strong-Beer*, beating Mr. *Wyley*'s Brown M. Mr. *Maſon*'s Bay M. *Beſſy-Bell*, Mr. *Nicholſon*'s Bay M. *Better-Luck*, Mr. *Ryley*'s Cheſ. G. *Have-at-'em.*

ROTHERHAM.

In the firſt Week in *September*, the following four ſtarted for a 10 *l.* Prize at *Rotherham*, 14 Hands, to carry 9 *ſt.* and to give or take, if higher or lower.

	1 H.	2 H.
Mr. *Wyley*'s Brown M. *Tripping-Nancy*	1	1
Mr. *Langley*'s Bay M. ———————	2	2
Mr. *Waters*'s Cheſ. M. ———————	3	3
Mr. 　　　　Grey M. ———————		

WAKEFIELD.

On the 7th Day of *September*, the following 3 ſtarted for a Prize, conſiſting of 14 Guineas, at *Wakefield, wt.* 10 *ſt.*

Mr.

	1 H.	2 H.	3 H.
Mr. *Witty*'s Grey G. *Pity-my-Condition* ——————	2	1	1
Sir *John Kaye*'s Bay G. —————	1	2	2
Mr. *Head*'s Chef. G. —————	dif		

This Prize was advertis'd to be 20 Guin. but a Chef. H. of Mr. *Vavafour*'s coming to ftart for it, the three abovemention'd refus'd to ftart againft him; upon which (in order to preferve the Sport of the Day) 'twas agreed to allow the faid Horfe of Mr. *Vavafour*'s a Premium of 6 Guin. out of the 20, on Condition that he would draw, and let the three mention'd above, run for the 14 Guineas that was the Remainder.

On the 9th *ditto*, on the fame Courfe, a Purfe of 15 Guin. was run for, being for Galloways, 9*f*. the higheft give and take, and won by

	1 H.	2 H.	3 H.
Mr. *Langley*'s Bay M. *Smiling-Betty*, 14 H. ——————	3	3	1
Mr. *Wyley*'s Brown M. —————	4	2	2
Mr. *Parfons*'s Bay M. —————	2	4	3
Mr. *Hedly*'s Bay M. —————	1	1	dif

PONTEFRACT.

On the 21ft Day of *September*, a Purfe of 15 Guin. was run for at *Pontefract*, free only for fuch Hunters, as never won 15 *l*. nor were in Sweats between the preceding *Michaelmas* and *Lady-Day*, *wt.* 12 *f*. 30 Shillings Entr. which Prize was won by

Mr.

	1 H.	2 H.
Mr. *Witty*'s Grey G. *Pity-my-Condition*	1	1
Mr. *Raven*'s Grey H. *Smiling-Tom*	2	2

On the fame Courfe, on the following Day, was 10 Guineas, for Galloways, 9 ß. the higheft give and take, one Guinea Entr. and won by

	1 H.	2 H.	3 H.
Mr. *Wyley*'s Bay M. *Tripping-Nancy*, 13 H. 3 I.	1	1	1
Mr. *Simpfon*'s Bay M. 13 H. ¼ I.	3	2	2
Mr. *Abbot*'s Chef. H. *Tantivy*, 13 H. 3 I. ½. ⅛	2	3	3

On the 23d *ditto*, on the fame Courfe, a free Purfe of 30 Guineas was run for, wt. 10 ß. 3 Guin. Entr. and won by

	1 H.	2 H.	3 H.
Mr. *Bright*'s Brown M. *Luna*	1	4	1
Mr. *Mountain*'s Grey H. *Fear-not*	4	1	2
Capt. *Gee*'s Bay H. *Bonny-Lad*	3	2	dr.
Mr. *Vavafor*'s Chef. H. *Sore-Heels*	2	3	dif
Mr. *Fifher*'s Chef. M. *Malton-Molly*	5	dif	

Enter for all three, on the 13th *ditto*; and 3 each Day were oblig'd to ftart.

BEDAL.

On the 30th Day of *September*, the Annual 30 Guin. Subfcription was run for at *Bedal*, being for 4 Year Olds, 9 ß. one Heat.

	1 H.	
Which Prize was won by Ld *Vane*'s Bay M.	1	

Mr.

	H.
Mr. *Hobson*'s Chef. M. ————	2
Mr. *Rakes Fulthorp*'s Bay M. ———	3
Mr. *Bathurst*'s Bay M. She fell, or had, 'tis said, certainly won }	4

On the following Day, on the same Course, a Purse of 20 *l*. Sterl. for 3 Year Olds was run for, *wt*. 8 *ft*. one 3 Miles Heat, and won by

	H.
Mr. *Proctor*'s Bay M. ————	1
Mr. *Lightfoot*'s Bay H. ————	2
Mr. *Collingwood*'s Bay H. ———	3
Col. *Graham*'s Chef. M. ———	4
Mr. *Rooke*'s Bay H. ———	5
Mr. *Johnson*'s Grey H. ———	6
Mr. *Pierce*'s Bay M. ———	7
Mr. *Close*'s Grey G. ———	8
Mr. *Stonehouse*'s Bay M. ———	9

A 3d and last Prize of this Meeting was a Purse of 10 Guineas, on the Day following, 14 Hands, to carry 9 *ft*. and to give or take, if higher or lower.

	1 H.	2 H.	3 H.	4 H.
This Prize was won by Capt. *Warlock*'s Chef. M. *Full-drive* }	1		3	1
Mr. *Routh*'s Chef. M. ———			1	2
Mr. *Tims*'s Chef. M. ———		1		3
Mr. *Binks*'s Bay M. ———	3	2	4	
Mr. *Furbank*'s Grey H. ———	2	dr.		
Mr. *Thornton*'s Bay M. ———	4	dr.		
Mr. *Hartly*'s Brown M. ———	5	dr.		
Mr. *Jefferson*'s Bay G. ———				
Mr. *Dixon*'s Chef. M. ———				
Mr. *Aiflaby*'s Chef. M. ———				

YARUM.

YARUM.

On the 13th Day of *October*, a 20 *l*. Purfe was run for at *Yarum*, free only for fuch as never won 20 Guin. in Plate, 14 Hands, to carry 10 *ft*. and to give or take, if higher or lower; Entr. 2 Guin. and won by

	1 H.	2 H.	3 H.
Mr. *Mayes*'s Grey H. *Bonny-Lad*, 14 H. ¼	5	1	1
Mr. *Thornton*'s Grey H. *Creeper*, 14 H.	1	3	3
Rev. Mr. *Tarran*'s Bay H. 14 H. 1 I. ½	2	2	2
Mr. *Witty*'s Grey G. *Pity-my-Con-dition*, 13 H. 3 I. ½	3	4	4
Mr. *Johnfon*'s Bay M. *Mifs-Hutton*, 13 H. 3 I.	4	dif	
Mr. *Bufter*'s Chef. H. 14 H. 1 I.	6	dif	
Capt. *Wickham*'s Chef. H. *Tria-contenti*, 13 H. 3 I. ½	dif		
Mr. *Weskew*'s Brown M. *Sweep-Stakes*, 14 H.	dif		

On the following Day, on the fame Courfe, was 15 *l*. Sterl. for 4 Year Olds, *wt.* 9 *ft*. 2 Miles at a Heat, one Guinea and a Half Entr.

	1 H.	2 H.
Which Prize was won by		
Mr. *Rakes Fulthorp*'s Bay M. got by *Young-Childers*	1	1
Mr. *Metcalf*'s Grey H. *Better-Luck*	3	2
Sir *John Stapylton*'s Grey M.	2	3

On the 15th *ditto*, on the fame Courfe, was a Purfe of 25 *l*. Sterl. for 5 Year Olds, *wt.* 10 *ft*. 2 Guin. and a Half Entr.

2   **Which**

Which Prize was won by	1 H.	2 H.	3 H.
Mr. *Solesby*'s Grey M. *Jenny-Nettle*	1	1	3
Mr. *Redshaw*'s Bay G.———	3	5	1
Mr. *Robinson*'s Grey M. *Mustard*——	5	2	2
Mr. *Cooke*'s Chef. H. *Royal-Colt* ——	2	3	6
Mr. *Rawlinson*'s Bay H. *Sprightly*——	4	4	4
Mr. *Grimes*'s Brown M. *Hopeless* ——	6	6	5
Mr. *Prisick*'s Bay H. *Merry-P*——le	7	dif	

BRIDLINGTON.

On the 21st Day of *October*. a 12 *l.* Plate for 4 Year Olds, was run for at *Bridlington*, wt. 9 st. 2 Miles at a Heat,

Which Prize was won by	1 H.	2 H.	3 H.
Mr. *Clank*'s Dun H. *Constant-Billy*——	3	1	1
Mr. *Wilders*'s Bay M. ———	1	2	2
Mr. *Body*'s Grey M. *Bridlington-Betty*	2	3	3

BRAMHAM-MOORE.

On the 1st Day of *November*, upon *Bramham-Moore*, Mr. *Laking*'s Chef. M. 9 st. 7 tb. got by *Johnson*'s *Turk*, beat Mr. *Middleton*'s Roan H. got by *Flower*, 10 st. 4 Miles, 20 Guin.

WALES,

WALES, 1731.

MONTGOMERYSHIRE, 1731.

WELCH-POOLE.

ON the 6th Day of *July*, a Purſe of 10 Guin. was run for at *Welch-Poole*, free only for ſuch ſix Year Olds, as never won 5 Guin. *wt.* 10 ſt. one Guin. Entr. Stakes for the 2d beſt.

	1 H.
This Prize was won by	
Mr. *Trevor*'s Dun G. *Harmleſs*————	1
Mr. *Williams*'s Bay G. *Chows*————	2

On the following Day, upon this Courſe, was 10 Guineas for Galloways, 9 ſt. the higheſt give and take, one Guin. Entr.

	1 H.	2 H.
This Prize was won by		
Mr. *Hurſt*'s Bay G. *Wanton-Willy*, 13 H.	1	1
3 I. $\frac{1}{2}$ ————		
Mr. *Hollant*'s Cheſ. M. *Creeping-Kate*	2	2

On the 8th *ditto*, on the ſame Courſe, a free Purſe of 20 Guin. was run for, *wt.* 11 ſt. 2 Guin. Entr. Stakes for the 2d beſt.

	1 H.
This Prize was won by	
Mr. *Williams Wynn*'s Bay H. *Spot*———	1
Mr. *Williams*'s Bay G. *Chows* ———	2

N

PEMBROKESHIRE, 1731.

HAVERFORD-WEST.

ON the 26th Day of *July*, a Purse of 27 Guin. was run for at *Haverford-West, wt.* 11 *st.* and won by

	1 H.
Mr. *Barlow*'s Strawberry H. *Dusty-Miller* ———	1
Mr. *Phillips*'s H. *Smoke-'em-Toper* ———	*dis*
Mr. *Edwards*'s M. *Smiling-Betty* ———	*dis*

On the same Course, on the 28th *ditto*, a Plate of upwards of 10 *l.* value was run for, being for Galloways, 9 *st.* the highest give and take, and own by

	1 H.	2 H.
Mr. *Barlow*'s Bay H. *Infant* ———	1	1
Mr. *Simmons*'s M. *Oxford-Lady* ———	2	2
Mr. *Loyd*'s M. *Smiling-Jenny* ———	*dis*	
Mr. *Ayleway*'s G. *Coney-skins* ———	*dis*	

COCK-

COCK-MATCHES, fought in 1731.

CAMBRIDGESHIRE.

AT *Newmarket*, in the *Easter* Week, *Hunting-donshire* fought *Cambridgeshire*, shewing 35 Cocks a side, for 6 Guineas and 100; in this Match was made 24 Battles, 15 of which were won by *Huntingdonshire*, and 9 by *Cambridgeshire*.

CUMBERLAND.

In the last Week in *July*, a Match was fought at the City of *Carlisle*, between Mr. *Philipson* and Mr. *Warwick*, shewing 31 Cocks a side, for 10 Guineas a Battle, and 100 Guineas the odd Battle; in which Match was 25 Battles, 13 of which were won by Mr. *Philipson*, and 12 by Mr. *Warwick*; this was a remarkably hard foughten Main, for it came to 12 and 12, and the 25th Battle was long, and strenuously contested on both Sides, but Mr. *Warwick*'s Cock at last gave it up, by actually running away.

DERBYSHIRE.

Near *Chesterfield*, on the 19th of *May*, Mr. *Street* fought Mr. *Buttering* 8 Shakebag Battles, for 5 Guineas and 10s. six of the eight being won by Mr. *Street*, and two by Mr. *Buttering*.

N 2   DEVON-

DEVONSHIRE.

At the City of *Exeter*, in the 1st Week in *March*, Col. *Hallet* fought Capt. *Newton*, shewing 31 Cocks a side, for 10 Guineas and 200; this Match was won by Col. *Hallet*, by several Battles.

COUNTY of DURHAM.

At *Darlington*, at *Shrove-Tide*, Capt. *Milbank* fought Mr. *Scafe*, shewing 21 Cocks a side, for 2 Guineas and 20; which Match was won by Capt. *Milbank* by 3 Battles.

At *Durham*, at the Time of the Races, Mr. *Smith* fought Mr. *Foster*, shewing 21 Cocks a side, for 2 Guineas and 10; in this Match was 12 Battles, Mr. *Smith* winning 9, and Mr. *Foster* 3.

LANCASHIRE.

In the *Easter-Week* at *Preston*, that Town fought the adjacent Country, shewing 41 Cocks a Side, for 2 Guineas and 20; in this Match was made 36 Battles, 19 of which were won by the Town, and 17 by the Country.

The same Parties, at the same Place, fought again in *July*, shewing 31 Cocks a side, for 4 Guin. and 40; in this Match were 22 Battles, 14 of which were won by the Country, and 8 by *Preston*.

At *Warrington*, in the last Week in *May*, Lancashire fought *Cheshire*, shewing 31 Cocks a side, for 10 Guineas and 100; in this Match was made 21 Battles, 12 of which were won by *Lancashire*, and 9 by *Cheshire*.

LEICES-

LEICESTERSHIRE.

In the Beginning of *May* at *Lutterworth*, Mr. *Peters* fought Mr. *Robinson*, shewing 21 Cocks a side, for a Guinea and 10; in this Match was 14 Battles, and each side won 7.

At *Earlshilton*, in the *Whitsun* Week, *Warwickshire* fought *Leicestershire*, shewing 31 Cocks a side, for 4 Guineas and 40; in this Match was 12 Battles, and each side won 6.

LINCOLNSHIRE.

At *Grimsthorp*, very early in the Spring, her Grace the Dutchess of *Ancaster* fought Mr. *Banks*, shewing 31 Cocks a side, for 20 Guineas and 200; in which Match were 20 Battles, 11 of which were won by her Grace, and 9 by Mr. *Banks*.

Her Grace also fought Mr. *Banks* at *Horncastle*, in the middle of *July*, shewing the same Number, for the same Sums; in this Match was 24 Battles, 14 of which were won by her Grace, and 10 by Mr. *Banks*.

MIDDLESEX.

In *London*, in the 1st Week in *February*, Mr. *Hickford* fought Capt. *Powers*, shewing 35 Cocks a side, for 2 Guineas and 20; this Match was won by Mr. *Hickford*, by 2 Battles.

At which Place, the succeeding Week, Mr. *Burdet* fought Mr. *Tasker*, shewing 35 Cocks a side, for 2 Guineas and 20; which Match was won by Mr. *Burdet*, by 2 Battles.

And also at the same Place, the 4th Week in *February*, Mr. *Sayer* fought Mr. *Smith*, shewing 35 a side for 6 Guineas and 100; this Match was won by Mr. *Sayer*, by 3 or 4 Battles.

In *London*, in the 1st Week in *March*, Mr. *Granger* fought Mr. *Hickford*, shewing 35 Cocks a side, for 10 Guineas and 200; this Match was won by Mr. *Granger*, by 5 or 6 Battles.

In the succeeding Week, at this Place, Mr. *Watson* fought Mr. *March*, shewing 35 Cocks a side, for 6 Guineas and 100; this Match was won by Mr. *Watson*, by 2 or 3 Battles.

And also at the same Place, the 4th Week in *March*, Mr. *Cope* fought Mr. *Smith*, shewing 35 a side, for 2 Guineas and 20; this Match was won by Mr. *Cope*, by 6 or 7 Battles.

And also in *London*, in the Month of *April*, Mr. *Tasker* fought Mr. *Burdet*, shewing 35 a side, all Staggs, for 4 Guineas and 40; this Match was won by Mr. *Tasker*, by 7 or 8 Battles.

At the same Place, the 1st Week in *July*, Mr. *Smith* shew'd 35 Cocks against Mr. *Crompton*, for 2 Guineas and 20; this Match was won by Mr. *Smith*, by 3 or 4 Battles.

NORFOLK.

At *Scole-Inn*, the first Week in *January*, *Norfolk* fought *Suffolk* for 3 Guineas a Battle; in which
Match

Match was made 28 Battles, 16 of which were won by *Norfolk*, and 12 by *Suffolk*.

At the same Place the first Week in *March*, *Suffolk* fought the City of *Norwich* for 5 Guineas a Battle; this Match also consisted of 28 Battles, 16 of which were won by *Suffolk*, and 12 by *Norwich*.

At this Place also, in the Beginning of *April*, *Norfolk* again fought *Suffolk* for 2 Guineas a Battle; in this Match was 26 Battles, and won by *Norfolk*, by 6 or 7 Battles.

In the Month of *May*, at this Place, *Norfolk* fought Mr. *Hammond* of *Suffolk*, for 3 Guineas a Battle; in which Match were 28 Battles, 16 of which were won by *Norfolk*, and 12 by Mr. *Hammond*.

In the middle of *June*, at this Place, *Norfolk* fought a Stagg Match against *Suffolk*, for 2 Guineas a Battle; making in the said Match 26 Battles, 15 of which were won by *Norfolk*, and 11 by *Suffolk*.

At *Holt*, in the Race Week, Mr. *Cony* fought Mr. *Workhouse*, shewing 21 Cocks a-side, for 5 Guineas and 50; in this Match was 13 Battles, 9 of which were won by Mr. *Cony*, and 4 by Mr. *Workhouse*.

NORTHUMBERLAND.

At *Newcastle* upon *Tyne*, in the *Easter* Week, Mr. *Smith* fought Mr. *Slater*, shewing 35 Cocks a-side, for 2 Guineas and 40; in which Match was 24 Battles, 19 of which were won by Mr. *Smith*, and 5 by Mr. *Slater*.

At

At this Place alſo, in the Race Week, Mr. *Lampton* fought Mr. *Philipſon*, ſhewing 31 Cocks a ſide, for 4 Guineas and 80; which Match was won by Mr. *Lampton*, by 3 Battles.

SOMERSETSHIRE.

At *Bath*, in the Month of *March*, that City fought the City of *Briſtol*, ſhewing 41 Cocks aſide, for 6 Guineas and 100; this Match was won by *Bath*, by 6 or 7 Battles.

At this City, in *May*, *Dorſetſhire* fought *Somerſetſhire*, ſhewing likewiſe 41 Cocks a ſide, for 6 Guineas and 100; which Match was won by *Dorſetſhire* by two Battles.

At this City in the ſucceeding *May* 1732, the Hon. Mr. *Greville* fights Mr. *Seger*, ſhewing 31 Cocks a ſide, for 6 Guineas and 100; but 'tis believ'd that, with relation to this Match, there will be a 2d Contract, obliging each Side to ſhew 45 Cocks inſtead of 31.

SURREY.

At *Epſom*, in the Beginning of *May* (being at the Time of the Races) Mr. *Smith* fought Col. *Butler*, ſhewing 35 Cocks a ſide, for 4 Guineas and 40; this Match was won by Mr. *Smith*, by 2 Battles.

At *Guildford*, at *Whitſuntide*, being the Time of the Races, *Reading* fought *Egham*, ſhewing 35 Cocks a ſide, for 2 Guineas and 20; in this Match was made 21 Battles, 11 of which were won by *Reading*, and 10 by *Egham*,

At *Camberwell*, in *July*, Mr. *Watson* fought Col. *Butler*, shewing 31 Cocks a side, for 2 Guineas and 20; this Match was won by Mr. *Watson*, by 2 or 3 Battles.

SUSSEX.

At *Arundel* in the 2d Week in *May*, that Town fought the City of *Chichester*, shewing 21 Cocks a side, for 2 Guineas and 20; this Match consisted of 15 Battles, 11 of which were won by *Arundel*, and 4 by *Chichester*.

At *Chichester*, in the middle of *June*, the same Parties fought again, shewing the same Numbers, for the same Sums; in which Match was 19 Battles, 12 of which were won by *Arundel*, and 7 by *Chichester*.

WILTSHIRE.

At *Salisbury*, in the 1st Week in *June*, *Somersetshire* fought *Wiltshire*, shewing 41 Cocks a side, for 6 Guineas and 100; this Match was won by *Somersetshire*, by 5 or 6 Battles.

YORKSHIRE.

At *Wakefield*, in the *Easter* Week, a Match was fought between that Town and Part of *Lancashire*, shewing 31 Cocks a side, for 5 Guineas and 50; in which Match was 20 Battles, and each side won 10.

At *Leeds*, in the 2d Week in *May*, Mr. *Horton* fought Mr. *Heber*, shewing 31 Cocks a side, for 4 Guin. and 40; in which Match was 19 Battles, 10 of which

which were won by Mr. *Horton*, and 9 by Mr. *Heber*.

In the *Whitſun* Week, at this Place, Mr. *Wilkinſon* fought *Rippon*, ſhewing 31 Cocks a ſide, for 4 Guineas and 40; in which Match was 25 Battles, 15 of which were won by Mr. *Wilkinſon*, and 10 by *Rippon*.

At *Beverly*, in the Race Week, that Town fought *Kingſton upon Hull*, ſhewing 31 Cocks a ſide, for 2 Guineas and 10; which Match was won by *Beverly*.

MATCHES,

MATCHES, &c. to be Run at *Newarket*.

April, 1732.

	Stones.	Pounds.	Miles.	Guineas.	Forfeits.
ON the 1st Day of this Month, the Duke of *Bolton*'s Chef. *Filly*, full Sister to *Sloven*, against Mr. *Henly*'s Bay *Filly*, out of the Dam of Sir *Robert Fagg*'s *Tickle-me-quickly*, and the *Walcot* Dun *Arabian* ———	8	5	4	200	Half.
On the 2d *ditto*, Duke of *Bolton*'s Chef. *Filly*, out of *Coquet* and *Bay-Bolton*, against Mr. *Henly*'s Chef. *Filly*, out of *Fenny-Fill* and the *Walcot* Grey *Arabian* ———	8	5	4	200	Half.
Same Day Earl of *Portmore*'s Brown *Filly*, got by the bald Galloway, 'gainst Mr. *How*'s Black Colt, got by his *Perfian* ———	8	7	4	200	50

3d.

	S.	P.	M.	G.	
3d *ditto*, Earl of *Hallifax*'s *Justice*, 8 *st*. 12 *l*. 'gainst Earl of *Portmore*'s *Daffidil*	8	5	4	200	Half.
4th *ditto*, Earl of *Portmore*'s *Victorious*, 9 *st*. 5 *l*. 'gainst Mr. *Coke*'s *Silver-Locks*———	8	1	5	200	Half.
On the *Friday* following, the 1st *Thursday* in this Month, Duke of *Bolton*'s *Fear-not*, 'gainst Mr. *Coke*'s *Hobgoblin*———	8	10	4	500	Half.
10th *ditto*, Earl of *Essex*'s Bay Filly, out of *Cream-Cakes* and the Earl of *Nottingham*'s *Arabian*, 'gainst Sir *Robert Fagg*'s Black *Filly*. The *Indian-Virgin*, out of a Sister to Ld *Onslow*'s *White-Foot*, and *Sore-Heels*———	8		4	200	Half.
12th *ditto*, Earl of *Essex*'s Grey *Filly*, out of *Countess* and the Earl of *Nottingham*'s *Arabian*, 'gainst Sir *Robert Fagg*'s Bay *Filly*, out of a *Bastow* Mare, and *Monkey*	8		4	200	Half.
13th *ditto*, Duke of *Bolton*'s *Younker*, 'gainst Mr. *Panton*'s *Mouse*———	8	5	4	300	Half.
22d *ditto*, Duke of *Bridgewater*'s Bay Colt 'gainst Earl of *Hallifax*'s Colt, out of the *Farmer-Mare* and Mr. *How*'s *Persian*———		7	4	200	Half. Oc-

October, 1732.

	S.	P.	M.	G.	F.

On the 1st Day of this Month, Duke of *Bridgewater*'s Chef. Colt, 'gainst Earl of *Portmore*'s Grey Colt, bought of Major *Gipps* —————

	S.	P.	M.	G.	F.
	8	7	4	200	Half.

On the *Tuesday* before the 1st *Thursday* in this Month, Earl of *Godolphin*'s Bay Colt, got by *Darice*, 'gainst Earl of *Hallifax*'s Bay Colt ————

	8	7	4	200	Half.

On the following Day, Duke of *Bolton*'s Black Colt, out of the Earl of *Bristol*'s Grey Mare, 'gainst Duke of *Devonshire*'s Brown Colt, out of *Cynder-Wench* ————

	8	7	4	200	Pay or Run.

Same Day, Earl of *Godolphin*'s Bay Colt, got by the bald Galloway, 'gainst Earl of *Hallifax*'s Chef. Colt, got by *Jigg* ————

	8	7	4	200	Half.

On the *Monday* after the 1st *Thursday* in this Month, the Duke of *Bolton* and the Earl of *Portmore* are each to start a Horse, Mare, or Gelding, being each of them respectively such as was the Owner's Property on the 17th of *April* 1730, being the Day of matching, and then rising 3 Years old ————

	8	7	4	200	Run or pay.

O

On

	S.	P.	M.	G.	F.
On the *Friday* after the 1ſt *Thurſday* in this Month, Duke of *Devonſhire*'s dark Bay Colt, 'gainſt Duke of *Bridgewater*'s Bay Colt ——	8	5	4	200	Half.
21ſt of this Month, Duke of *Bolton*'s *Fear-not*, 'gainſt Mr *Panton*'s *Mouſe* ——	7	5	4	500	Run or Pay.

April, 1733.

	S.	P.	M.	G.	F.
On the 1ſt Day of this Month, Duke of *Bridgewater*'s Bay Colt, call'd *Beauty*, 'gainſt Ld Viſcount *Lonſdale*'s Bay Colt, call'd *Ugly*, 8 ſt 7 *l.* the higheſt give and take			4	200	Half.
Same Day, Earl of *Portmore*'s Bay Colt, got by *Fox*, 'gainſt Earl of *Hallifax*'s Filly, out of the *Farmer-Mare*, and Mr. *How*'s *Perſian*, 8 ſt. the higheſt give and take ——			4	200	Half.
Same Day, Ld Viſcount *Lonſdale*'s Bay *Filly*, out of a Mare bought of Ld *Darcy*, and his Lordſhip's *Arabian*, 'gainſt Mr. *Panton*'s *Filly*, out of the Duke of *Rutland*'s *Ebony-Mare*, and got by *Childers* ——	8	2	4	200	Half.
13th *ditto*, Duke of *Bolton*'s *Cyſax*, 'gainſt Mr. *Panton*'s *Vulcan* ——	8	5	4	300	Half.

I

24th

	S.	P.	M.	G.	F.
24th *ditto*, Duke of *Bolton's Befs-a-Bell*, 8*ft.* 5*l.* 'gainft Earl of *Portmore's Mandane*	8	2	4	200	Pay or Run,
Same Day, Earl of *Hallifax's* Colt, got by *Bumper*, and out of a half-Sifter to the fame, 'gainft Ld Vifc. *Middleton's* Colt, out of a Mare of his Lordfhip's own, and got by *Figg* ———	8	5	4	100	Pay or Run.

October, 1733.

	S.	P.	M.	G.	F.
1ft of this Month, Earl of *Godolphin's* Bay Colt, 'gainft the Earl of *Portmore's* Chef. Colt, bought of the *Grecians* at *Hyde-Park-Corner*, and got by *Fox* ———	8	7	4	300	Half.
3d *ditto*, Earl of *Godolphin's* Chef. Colt, out of the *Stanhope* Mare and the bald Galloway, 'gainft Earl of *Portmore's* Grey Colt, out of *Mifs-Metcalf* and *Fox*; the higheft to carry 8*ft.* 7 *lb.* the loweft———	8	3	4	300	Half.
On the *Wednefday* before the 1ft *Thurfday* in this Month, Duke of *Bolton's* Bay Colt, out of the Earl of *Briftol's* Grey Mare, 'gainft Duke of *Devonfhire's* Bay Colt, out of the Ebony Mare ———	8	7	4	200	Half.
					On

April, 1734.

	S.	P.	M.	G.	F.
On the 1ſt Day of this Month, Duke of *Bolton*'s Cheſ. *Filly*, out of *Coquet* and *Bay-Bolton*, 'gainſt Earl of *Portmore*'s Cheſ. *Filly*, out of the Bay *Arabian* Mare and *Bay-Wilkinſon*	8	5	4	300	Half.
On the *Wedneſday* before the firſt *Thurſday* in this Month, a Bay *Filly* of the Duke of *Bridgewater's*, a Colt of the Earl of *Portmore's*, out of *Miſs-Hen*, and a Bay *Filly* of the Ld *Gower's*, out of the Dam of *Duſty-Miller* and *Slouch*, are match'd to run for 200 Guineas each, Half Forfeit	8	4	4	200	Half.
On the *Saturday* after the firſt *Thurſday* in this Month, Earl of *Godolphin*'s Bay Colt, full Brother to *White-Foot*, againſt Mr. *Panton*'s Grey Colt	8	7	4	300	Half.
10th *ditto*, Earl of *Portmore's* Cheſ. Colt, out of *Alba-Jenny*, 'gainſt Sir *Rob.Fagg*'s Cheſ. *Filly*, bought of Mr. *Crofts*, and got by *Sore-Heels*	8	2	4	200	Half.

Octo-

October, 1734.

	S.	P.	M.	G.	F.
On the 1st Day of this Month, Earl of *Portmore*'s *Filly*, out of *Miss-Medcalf* and the Dun *Arabian*, 'gainst Mr. *How*'s Colt, out of his Black *Barb.* Mare and *Young-Spark* ——	8	7	4	200	Half.
On the following Day, Duke of *Bolton*'s Chef. *Filly*, out of *Coquet* and *Bay-Bolton*, 'gainst Earl of *Portmore*'s Colt, out of the Dam of *Victorious* and *Greyhound* ——	8	7	4	200	Pay or Run.
On the *Saturday* after the first *Thursday* in this Month, Ld *Onslow*'s Bay Colt, 'gainst Mr. *Walker*'s Colt ——	8	7	4	200	Half.
22d *ditto*, Duke of *Bolton*'s Chef. *Filly*, 'gainst Mr. *Panton*'s Chef. *Filly* ——	8	5	4	200	Half.
One Day in this Month, Duke of *Bridgewater*'s Bay Colt, out of *Newmarket-Betty*; Earl of *Portmore*'s Chef. Colt, out of the Chef. *Arabian* Mare, bought at *Hyde-Park-Corner*; Sir *Michael Newton*'s Bay *Filly*, out of *Proserpine* and Sir *Michael*'s own *Arabian*; and a Chef. *Filly* of Mr. *Panton*'s, out of the *Confederate-Filly* and	8	5	4	400	Half,

O 3

Childers;

Childers; are match'd to run one four Miles Heat for 100 Guineas each, Half Forfeit

April, 1735.

	F.	G.	M.	P.	S.

On the *Monday* before the 1st *Thursday* in this Month, Earl of *Essex's* Chel. *Filly*, Earl of *Hallifax's* Brown *Filly*, got by the young *Mountain Arabian* at *Hampton-Court*; Ld Viscount *Middleton's* Brown *Filly*, out of a *Barb.* Mare, and a Bay Colt of Sir *Michael Newton's*, out of *Grey-Molly* and Sir *Michael's* own *Arabian*, are match'd to run one 4 Miles Heat for 100 Guineas each

Run or Pay. | 400 | 4 | | 8 |

October, 1735.

On the 1st Day of this Month, Duke of *Bolton's* Colt, out of *Coquet* and *Bay-Bolton*, 'gainst the Duke of *Devonshire's* Colt, out of the *Ebony* Mare and *Childers* ——

Half. | 300 | 4 | 7 | 8 |

On the *Friday* following the 1st *Thursday* in this Month, Sir *Robert Fagg's* Chel. Colt, 'gainst Mr. *Elstob's* Chel. *Filly*, got by *Almanzor* ——

Half. | 200 | 4 | 12 | 8 |

26th

	S.	P.	M.	G.	F.
26th *ditto*, Earl of *Portmore's* Foal, out of the Dam of *Victorious*, 'gainst Mr. *Fauquier's* Foal, out of a Sister to *Country-Wench* and *Partner* ——————	9		4	200	Half.
Same Day, Earl of *Portmore's* Colt, out of the Dam of *Victorious* and *Partner*; Mr. *Fauquier's* Colt, out of a Sister to *Country-Wench* and *Partner*; and Mr. *Elstob's* Chef. *Filly*, got by *Almanzor*; are match'd to run one four Miles Heat for 200 Guineas each, Half Forfeit	9		4	200	Half.

April, 1736.

	S.	P.	M.	G.	F.
2d Day of this Month, Mr. *Lechmere's* Foal, out of *Ebony* and *Crab*, 'gainst Mr. *Fauquier's* Foal, out of a Sister to *Country-Wench* and *Smiling-Tom* ——————	9		4	100	
On the *Saturday* after the 1st *Thursday* in this Month, Duke of *Bolton's* Colt Fole, out of *Coquet* and *Bay-Bolton*, 'gainst Earl of *Portmore's* Colt Foal, out of the Dam of *Victorious* and *Partner* ——————	8	7	4	200	Half.

P R O.

PROPOSALS

For Printing by

Subscription,

Once a Year for 7 Years successively,

AN Historical LIST of all Horse-Matches run, and of all Plates and Prizes run for in *England*, of the Value of Ten Pounds and upwards, in each particular Year of the seven preceding the Publication of each Book.

Containing the Name of the Owner of each Horse, Mare, or Gelding, that run as above, and Names and Colours of the said Horses also.

With the Winner distinguish'd of every Match, Plate, Prize, or Stakes; the Weight that's carry'd at every Place of Running, the Size that Galloways, &c. are measur'd to, and the Places in which the losing Horses come in: To which will annually be added, a List of the principal Cock-Matches of the respective Year, and who were the Winners and Losers of them, &c.

This

This Work will be publish'd every Year about *Christmas*, for seven Years successively, beginning in 1727.

As the same appearing *annually* in the midst of Winter, will be an agreeable Amusement in that dull unactive Season, rendring Gentlemen capable, even in their Chambers, of diverting themselves with a Prospect, as it were, of the Sport of each past Year; so also must the Advantage be considerable in point of Practice, each Book discovering what Horses are moving in all Parts of the Kingdom, and what Figure every particular one of 'em has made at the Places of his Running the Season before; what Alterations, different Weights, or different Courses, or different Seasons of the Year has caus'd in any of them. From hence 'twill be always discoverable what old Horses are dropping, and how they decline and go off; what young Horses are every Year coming up; and by what Steps they advance and improve, &c. Which must render Gentlemen capable of reducing their Calculations nearer to Perfection, and consequently of Matching or Betting with greater Advantage.

The Conditions are, That Half-a-Crown be paid at Subscribing, and Five Shillings annually, in the said seven Years, at the delivery of a Book, the last Year only excepted, in which only Half-a-Crown is to be paid; which, with the Half-Crown receiv'd in hand, will make Five Shillings for the last, or seventh Book.

Notice will annually be given in the Papers as soon as the Work is printed, and where, in *London*, ready to be deliver'd out,

By JOHN CHENY.

N.B.

N.B. The foregoing Book is the fifth of the Seven, of which a Number is printed more than are subscribed for; with which any Gentleman, *&c.* may be furnish'd, if pleas'd to subscribe for the two succeeding ones also.

SUBSCRIPTIONS are taken in by Mr. *Roger Williams*, at his Coffee-House in *St. James's-street*; by Mr. *Feales*, Bookseller, at *Rowe's-Head* in *St. Clement's Church-Yard* in the *Strand, London*; by the said *John Cheny*, as he travels to take his Accounts; and at Inns, Coffee-Houses, *&c.* in most of the Towns in *England.*

SUB-

SUBSCRIBERS NAMES.

HIS Grace the Duke of *Norfolk.*
His Grace the Duke of *Somerset.*
His Grace the Duke of *Richmond.*
His Grace the Duke of *Bolton.*
His Grace the Duke of *Leeds.*
His Grace the Duke of *St. Albans.*
His Grace the Duke of *Bedford.*
His Grace the Duke of *Devonshire.*
His Grace the Duke of *Rutland.*
His Grace the Duke of *Hamilton* and *Brandon.*
His Grace the Duke of *Montrose.*
His Grace the Duke of *Queensberry.*
His Grace the Duke of *Kent.*
His Grace the Duke of *Ancaster.*
His Grace the Duke of *Manchester.*
His Grace the Duke of *Bridgewater.*

Right Hon. the Lord Marquis of *Carmarthen.*
Right Hon. the Lord Marquis of *Carnarvan.*

Right Hon. the Earl of *Derby.*
Right Hon. the Earl of *Huntingdon.*
Right Hon. the Earl of *Exeter.*
Right Hon. the Earl of *Essex.*
Right Hon. the Earl of *Cardigan.*
Right Hon. the Earl of *Carlisle.*

P   Right

Right Hon. the Earl of *Litchfield*.
Right Hon. the Earl of *Gainsborough*.
Right Hon. the Earl of *Scarborough*.
Right Hon. the Earl of *Albemarle*.
Right Hon. the Earl of *Godolphin*.
Right Hon. the Earl of *Oxford*.
Right Hon. the Earl of *Tankerville*.
Right Hon. the Earl of *Hallifax*.
Right Hon. the Earl of *Crawford*.
Right Hon. the Earl of *Hume*.
Right Hon. the Earl of *Portmore*.
Right Hon. the Earl of *Thomond*.
Right Hon. the Earl of *Barrymore*.

Right Hon. the Lord *William Beauclerck*
Right Hon. the Lord *Harry Powlet*.
Right Hon. the Lord *Naſſaw Powlet*.
Right Hon. the Lord *William Mannors*.
Right Hon. the Lord *Lindſey*.
Right Hon. the Lord *William Hamilton*.
Right Hon. the Lord Viſcount *Fowler Fauconberg*.
Right Hon. the Lord Viſcount *Lonſdale*.
Right Hon. the Lord Viſcount *Preſton*.
Right Hon. the Lord Viſcount *Primeroſe*.
Right Hon. the Lord Viſcount *Cullen*.
Right Hon. the Lord Viſcount *Middleton*.
Right Hon. the Lord Viſcount *Molyneux*.
Right Hon. the Lord Viſcount *Howe*.
Right Hon. the Lord Viſcount *Tyrconnel*.
Right Hon. the Lord Viſcount *Gage*.

Right Hon. the Lord *Abergavenny*.
Right Hon. the Lord *Lewiſham*.
Right Hon. the Lord *Brudenell*.
Right Hon. the Lord *Garlies*.
Right Hon. the Lord *Milſingtown*.
Right Hon. the Lady *Milſingtown*.
Right Hon. the Lord *Boyle*.
Right Hon. the Lord *Darcy*.   Right

Right Hon. the Lord *Dudley* and *Ward.*
Right Hon. the Lord *Craven.*
Right Hon. the Lord *Gower.*
Right Hon. the Lord *Cadogan.*
Right Hon. the Lord *Walpole.*
Right Hon. the Lord *Malton.*
Right Hon. the Lord *Somerville.*
Right Hon. the Lord *Mordaunt.*
Right Hon. the Lord Baron *Swartz.*

Hon. *William Cecil* Efq;
Hon. *Charles Fielding* Efq;
Hon. *James Brudenell* Efq;
Hon. *John Spencer* Efq;
Hon. *Fuller Craven* Efq;
Hon. *Henry Howard* Efq;
Hon. *Edward Leigh* Efq;
Hon. *Thomas Leigh* Efq;
Hon. *Rathwell Willobough* Efq;
Hon. *Bar. Afhburnham* Efq;
Hon. *Henry Vane* Efq;
Hon. *William Levefon Gower* Efq;
Hon. *Thomas Levefon Gower* Efq;
Hon. *Thomas Noel* Efq;
Hon. *Henry Howard* Efq;
Hon. *Richard Butler Mt. Garret* Efq;
Hon. *Carryl Molyneux* Efq;

Sir *Thomas Grefley* Bart.
Sir *Mar. Wyvill* Bart.
Sir *John Egerton* Bart.
Sir *Cecil Bifhop* Bart.
Sir *Richard Grofvenor* Bart.
Sir *Arthur Haflerige* Bart.
Sir *Edward Stanley* Bart.
Sir *John Kaye* Bart.
Sir *Cloberry Noel,* Bart.

Sir

Sir *John Swinburn* Bart.
Sir *Nathaniel Curzon* Bart.
Sir *Henry Slingsby* Bart.
Sir *James Pennyman* Bart.
Sir *William St. Quintin* Bart.
Sir *Edward Blount* Bart.
Sir *Carnaby Haggerſten* Bart.
Sir *Nev. Hickman* Bart.
Sir *William Strickland* Bart.
Sir *Fra. Edwards* Bart.
Sir *Henry Atkins* Bart.
Sir *William Middleton* Bart.
Sir *John Stapylton* Bart.
Sir *Wool. Dixie* Bart.
Sir *Robert Fagg* Bart.
Sir *Thomas Frankland* Bart.
Sir *John Aſtly* Bart.
Sir *Darcy Dawes* Bart.
Sir *Verny Cave* Bart.
Sir *Ralph Aſhton* Bart.
Sir *Francis Skipwith* Bart.
Sir *Walter Hawkſworth* Bart.
Sir *Edward Blacket* Bart.
Sir *Thomas Samwell* Bart.
Sir *Thomas Hobby* Bart.
Sir *William Milner* Bart.
Sir *Jo. Buckworth* Bart.
Sir *Charles Sedley* Bart.
Sir *Compton Domvile* Bart.
Sir *Robert S. Cotton* Bart.
Sir *Thomas Peyton* Bart.
Sir *Jonathan Jenkinſon* Bart.
Sir *Edward Gaſcoigne* Bart.
Sir *John Chaplin* Bart.
Sir *Euſ. Buzwell* Bart.
Sir *Cordell Firebraſs* Bart.
Sir *Peter Soame* Bart.
Sir *Edward Stradling* Bart.

Sir

Sir *Thomas Lowther* Bart.
Sir *Windsor Hunlocke* Bart.
Sir *Reginald Greham* Bart.
Sir *William Wolseley* Bart.
Sir *Fra. Anderton* Bart.
Sir *Hen. Inglefield* Bart.
Sir *John Chester* Bart.
Sir *John Morgan* Bart.
Sir *George Wynn* Bart.
Sir *Edward O'Brien* Bart.
Sir *Thomas Reynell* Bart.
Sir *Richard Osbaldiston* Knt.

Sir *William Stanhope* Knight of the *Bath.*
Sir *Charles Wills* Knight of the *Bath.*
Sir *Mich. Newton* Knight of the *Bath.*
Sir *William Morgan* Knight of the *Bath.*

Hon. Col. *Howard.*
Hon. Col. *Handesyd*
Hon. Col. *Lee.*
Hon. Col. *Whitworth.*
Hon. Col. *Host.*

BEDFORDSHIRE.
JOHN *Reynolds* Esq;
Charles *Palmer* Esq;

BUCKS.
Richard *Lowndes* Esq;

BERKS.
William *Gore* Esq;
Samuel *Lintel* Esq;
Thomas *Lawrance* Esq;
John *Stonehouse* Esq;
John *Sake* Esq;
Cherry *Hays* Esq;
Hen. *Pye, jun.* Esq;
Thomas *Garrard* Esq;
Mr. *Nun*
Mr. *Roberts*
Mrs. *Stret*

CAMBRIDGESHIRE.
Richard *Little* Esq;
Philip *Life* Esq;
William *Craven* Esq;
Soame *Jenyns* Esq;
Tho. *Wrighte* Esq;
Mr. *Shade*
Mr. *Darling*
Mr. *Pitt*
Mr. *White*
Mr. *Whitaker*
Mr. *Ball*

CHESHIRE.
John *Egerton* Esq;
Thomas *Grosvenor* Esq;
William *Stanly* Esq;
Robert *Cholmondeley* Esq;
Robert *Davis* Esq;
William *Brinkir* Esq;
Thomas *Chetham* Esq;
Ralph *Horton* Esq;
William *Glegg* Esq;
Robert *Pigot* Esq;
Mr. *Old*
Mr. *Horton*
Mr. *Potter*
Mr. *Poole*
Mr. *Burton*
Mr. *Taply*
Mr. *Smith*
Mr. *Bruce*
Mr. *Sigwick*
Mr. *Parker*
Mr. *Ruston*

CUMBERLAND.
Thomas *Howard* Esq;
Francis *Warwick* Esq;
Thomas *Salkeld* Esq;
Capt. *Crosby*
Mr. *Pattinson* at the *Grapes*
   in *Carlise*

DERBYSHIRE.
Rev. Mr. *Simpson*
Littleton P. *Meynell* Esq;
                 Geo.

Geo. Venables Vernon Esq;
Edward Bret. Bainbrigge Esq;
Christopher Horton Esq;
Samuel Alleyne Esq;
John Wooley Esq;
G. Meynell Esq;
Hen. Weltden Esq;
Thomas Bagshaw Esq;
Ger. Rosell Esq;
Ger. Balguy Esq;
Hen. Bourne Esq;
Robert Bateman Esq;
Geo. Mower Esq;
N. Thornhill Esq;
Pat. Chaworth Esq;
Richard Hawley Esq;
Brooke Boothby Esq;
Tho. Barker Esq;
Mr. Froggat
Mr. Milns
Mr. Taylor
Mr. Bright
Mr. Street
Mr. Cartwright
Mr. Gibbon
Mr. Hardgrave

John Hornywood Esq;
——— Collingwood Esq;
G. Vane Esq;
Thomas Charlton Esq;
Robert Chilton Esq;
Nich. Lampton Esq;
Hen. Lampton Esq;
John Morland Esq;
John Lamb Esq;
Jo. Nesham Esq;
Tho. Billings Esq;
Mr. Philipson
Mr. Dun
Mr. Jackson
Mr. White
Mr. Fulthorp
Mr. Stevenson
Mr. Tinker
Mr. Peacock
Mr. Steel
Mr. Campbell
Mr. Gibson
Mr. Scafe
Mr. Sigwick
Mr. Mowbray
Mr. Wilkinson
Mr. Hirdman
Mr. Smith

DEVONSHIRE.
John Bampfield Esq;

COUNTY DURHAM.
Meyburn Smith Esq;
——— Davinson Esq;
George Bows Esq;
Ralph Jennison Esq;
Jo. Millits Esq;
Ralph Keling Esq;

DORSETSHIRE.
Thomas Fowns Esq;
Tho. Hoddy Esq;

ESSEX.
John Howe Esq;
John Barefoot Esq;
Wroth Stern, Esq;
Carteret Leathes Esq;
William Peck Esq;

Ran-

Randyll Peck Efq;
George Griffin Efq;
William Ruffel Efq;
Mr. Patch
Mr. Woodcock
Mr. Fryar

GLOUCESTERSHIRE.
John Howe Efq;
Berk. Freeman Efq;
Mr. Kirby
Mr. Parry

HAMPSHIRE.
Anthony Henly Efq;
Ellis St. John Efq;
Richard Cowper Efq;
John Belfon Efq;
Robert Forder Efq;
John Cope Efq;
Edw. Thomas Williamfon Efq;
———— Willis Efq;
Mr. Goldney
Mr. Butler
Mr. Chitty
Mr. Buft

HERTFORDSHIRE.
Charles Cafar, jun. Efq;
Thomas Sere Efq;
Capt. Crouch
Mr. Moor
Mr. Cock
Mr. Edwards
Mr. Elmy at the Mitre in Barnet

Mr. Holmes at the Green Man in Barnet
Mr. Faman

HEREFORDSHIRE.
Vel. Cornewall Efq;
Scud. Lechmere Efq;
John Driver Efq;
Mr. Bennet

HUNTINGTONSHIRE.
Thomas Hals Efq;
Mr. Darlow
Mr. Whetham

KENT.
Mr. Bellamy
Mr. Harrifon
Mr. Weft

LANCASHIRE.
Ban. Parker Efq;
Hen. Walton Efq;
Richard Allen Efq;
Thomas Hesketh Efq;
William Cowper Efq;
John Trafford Efq;
Ralph Standifh Howard Efq;
Richard Townly Efq;
Thomas Standifh Efq;
Roger Noel Efq;
William Clayton Efq;
Richard Molyneux Efq;
Edward Dicconfon Efq;
Ralph Taylor Efq;
Mr. Ireland
Mr. Cafe

Mr.

Mr. *Makin*
Mr. *Darbyshire*
Mr. *Dean*
Mr. *Sharpless*
Mr. *Addison*
Mr. *Knight*
Mr. *Wagstaff*
Mr. *Bracken*
Mr. *Williams*
Mr. *Runegar*
Mr. *Hodges*

LEICESTERSHIRE.
Thomas Boothby Efq;
James Winstanly Efq;
Edward Smith Efq;
Leonard Piddock Efq;
Thomas Plampin Efq;
James Burflem Efq;
Waring Ashby Efq;
Thomas Noble Efq;
Edward Munday Efq;
William Ruding Efq;
Cheverton Hartop Efq;
Edward Pigland Efq;
Mr. *Swan*
Mr. *Farmer*
Mr. *Annis*
Mr. *Stubbs*
Mr. *Smith*
Mr. *Wright*
Mr. *Bass*
Mr. *Farmer*
Mr. *Sabine*
Mr. *Bass*
Mr. *Peters*

LINCOLNSHIRE.
Rev. Mr. *Cawthorn*

Rev. Mr. *Stafford*
Thomas Heneage Efq;
Fra. Anderfon Efq;
C. Pelham Efq;
Cha. Hall Efq;
Mathew Lifter Efq;
—— *Medly* Efq;
Richard Hardwick Efq;
James Bateman Efq;
William Goodhall Efq;
Edmund White Efq,
Nich. Bard. Emerfon Efq;
Edward Afcoughe Efq;
Edward Wilfon Efq;
M. Humberftone Efq;
George Heneage Efq;
John Maddifon Efq;
Jo. Newton Efq;
James Fifh Efq;
Fitz. White Efq;
—— *Fowler* Efq;
Tho Trollope Efq;
Bar. Maffenberg Efq;
Blifs Pakey Efq;
Sam. Woolmer Efq;
Will. Alcock, jun. Efq;
Francis Parker Efq;
William Bedford Efq;
Tracy Pauncefort Efq;
Jo. Green Efq;
Clement Tudway Efq;
Charles Kirkham Efq;
John Cotton Efq;
Vincent Grantham Efq;
Thomas Parkin Efq;
Henry Obrien Efq;
Mr. *Hare*

Mr.

Mr. Bowers
Mr. Collingwood
Mr. Deighton
Mr. Alcock
Mr. Wanless
Mr. Smith
Mr. Lindsey
Mr. Colson
Mr. Hallum
Mr. Pell
Mr. Hurst
Mr. Bowers
Mr. Cowdron
Mr. Harrymet
Mr. Gibbons
Mr. Jackson
Mr. Ingram
Mr. Headen
Mr. Gundaymere
Mr. Chambers
Mr. Wooden
Mr. Dixon
Mr. Blithe
Mr. Beverly
Mr. Rawson
Mr. Howitt

MIDDLESEX.

Plukenett Woodroffe Esq;
Jona. Holloway Esq;
Joshua Smith Esq;
Tho. Bladen Esq;
William Cartwright Esq;
Richard Colliford Esq;
John Cotten Esq;
Hon. Rich. Arundel Esq;
Philip Southcott Esq.

Tho. Archer Esq;
Leigh Masters Esq;
Robert Burletson Esq;
Charles Slingsby Esq;
Kell Courtney Esq;
——— Hodges Esq;
William James Esq;
Ja. Russel Stapleton Esq;
George Shirly Esq;
Essex Meryicke Esq;
Richard Madan Esq;
Thomas Walker Esq;
Walter Tankred Esq;
Jo. Hanbury, jun. Esq;
William Walton Esq;
John Nut Esq;
Edw. Coke Esq;
J. Banks Esq;
Everard Buckworth Esq;
Henry Bromly Esq;
Francis Fauquier Esq;
James Seamer Esq;
John Rich Esq;
Thomas Panton Esq;
Joseph Philips Esq;
Thomas Backwell Esq;
Thomas Dean Esq;
William Murden Esq;
Tinningham Backwell Esq;
Thomas Boucher Esq;
——— Pierson Esq;
John Potter Esq;
Robert Hadsley Esq;
Thomas Burton Esq;
William Aglionby Esq;
William Rollison Esq;
Samuel Gumly Esq;

Richard

Richard Pate Esq;
William Sadler Esq;
Alexander Bell Esq;
Mr. Stevens
Capt. Bridge
Mr. Legg
Capt. Salmon
Mr. Scarlet
Mr. Harwood
Capt. Heard
Capt. Hill
Mr. Williams
Mr. Wotton
Mr. Danlow
Mr. Langhorn
Mr. Thornton
Mr. Gibson
Mr. Roch
Mr. Hall
Mr. Barnet
Mr. Grisewood
Mr. Gray
Mr. Brown
Mr. Edwards
Mr. Pace
Mr. Masters
Mr. Morris
Mr. Pate
Mr. Bently
Mr. Coffin
Mr. Morris
Mr. Gregg
Mr. Collins
Mr. Skelding
Mr. Moore
Mr. Robinson
Mr. Froling
Mr. Smith

Mr. Fosser
Mr. Winterton
Mr. Hollinshead
Mr. Hutchens
Mr. Ramsey
Mr. Elliot
Mr. Lukup
Mr. Tuffnel
Mr. Ovington
Mr. Kirby
Mr. Jones
Mr. Tomlinson
Mr. Gilder
Mr. Bennet
Mr. Stacy
Mr. Weekly
Mr. Clarke
Mr. Baynes at the Prince
    William Tavern, Cha-
    ring Cross
Mr. Holland
Mr. Williams
Mr. Seabrook
Mr. Millar
Mr. Audle
Mr. Hardy
Mr. Ankiece
Mr. Kite
Mr. Watson
Mr. Mascal
Mr. Worsley
Mr. Chapman
Mr. Canby
Mr. Eiley
Mr. Lucas
Mr. Wodman
Mr. Tatler
Mr. Adcock

Mr.

Mr. *Clarke*, at the *Three Pigeons* in *Brentford*
Mr. *Aldwell*
Mr. *Stacy*
Mr. *Harris*
Mr. *Clarke*
Mr. *Fifield*
Mr. *Try*
Mr. *Wood*
Mr. *Smith*
Mr. *Eland*
Mr. *Lowe*
Mr. *Green*
Mr. *Roberts*
Mr. *Hughs*
Mr. *Emerson*
Mr. *Kentishbare*
Mr. *Thurston*
Mr. *Peppercorn*
Mr. *Wilkins*

MONMOUTHSHIBE.
Robert *Hughs* Efq;
Richard *Jones* Efq;
W. *Watkin* Efq;
Mr. *Scudamore*

NORFOLK.
Benjamin *Bromhead* Efq;
Edwin *Cony* Efq;
Seaborne *Seman* Efq;
Robert *Suckling* Efq;
Caleb *Elwin* Efq;
John *Dethick* Efq;
William *Newman* Efq;
Hen. *Baynes* Efq;
Tho. *Upwood* Efq;

Capt. *Hoft*
Mr. *Manning*
Mr. *Martin*
Mr. *Richards*
Mr. *Brown*
Mr. *Wright*
Mr. *Kettle*
Mr. *Rayner*
Mr. *Large*
Mr. *Cleever*
Mr. *Catton*

NORTHAMPTONSHIRE.
Robert *Andrew* Efq;
Charles *Isham* Efq;
———— *Grice* Efq;
Henry *Stratford* Efq;
Edw. *Clarke* Efq;
Richard *Cumberland* Efq;
Charles *Kirkham* Efq;
Lucy *Knightly* Efq;
Cha. *Gore* Efq;
John *Rowel* Efq;
Mr. *Peach*
Mr. Quarter-Mafter *Burton*
Mr. *Peach*
Mr. *Philips*
Mr. *Charlsworth*
Mr. *Dicie*
Mr. *Bulmar*
Mr. *Smith*
Mr. *Leggat*
Mr. *Hall*
Mr. *Lovel*
Mr. *Thompson*
Mr. *Day*

Mr.

Mr. *Dunkley*
Mr. *Lemon*
Mr. *Smith*

NORTHUMBERLAND.

Walter Blacket Efq;
John Fenwick Efq;
Edward Haggerften Efq;
William Ogle Efq;
Thomas Errington Efq;
Thomas Lifle Efq;
Francis Wood Efq;
Robert Midford Efq;
William Carr Efq;
Henry Jenifon Efq;
John Stevenfon Efq;
William Wilkie Efq;
Alexander Hay Efq,
Robert Elrington Efq;
Reynold Hall Efq;
John Charlton Efq;
Mr. *Baltran*
Mr. *Waugh*
Mr. *Wood*
Mr. *Twizle*
Mr. *Armftrong*
Mr. *Pratt*
Mr. *Bulman*
Mr. *Downs*

NOTTINGHAMSHIRE,

M. Mufters Efq;
Ed. Poole Efq;
J. Digby Efq;
Langford Collins Efq;
Borlace Warren Efq;
L. Rollifton Efq;
Mr. *Fifher*

Mr. *Sully*
Mr. *Peyntell*
Mr. *Shore*
Mr. *Tomlinfon*
Mr. *Richard Semer*
Mr. *Dickinfon*
Mr. *Robfon*
Mr. *Powell*

OXFORDSHIRE.

Rob. Dafhwood, jun. Efq;
John Keck Efq;
Jo. Pitt Efq;
James Dawkins Efq;
R. M. Bray Efq;
George Kendrick Efq;
Mr. *Thatcher*
Mr. *Bradfhaw*
Mr. *Underwood*
Mr. *Heighfield*
Mr. *Gibbons*

SHROPSHIRE.

Stephen Cotton Efq;
Andrew Charlton Efq;
St. John Charlton Efq;
Anthony Hill Efq;
Herbert Mackworth Eq;
Richard Syer Efq;
Robert Piget Efq;
Capt. *Pye*
Mr. *Corbet*
Mr. *Gelding*
Mr. *Mafon*
Mr. *Stacey*

SOMERSETSHIRE.

John Periam Efq;
Q   T. *White*

T. White Esq;
Joseph Langton Esq;
J. Harrington Esq;
J. Wright Esq;
Philip Bennet Esq;
Richard Chester Esq;
Jos. Moore Esq;
Tho. Try Esq;
Cha. Estcourt Esq;
William Monk Esq;
Edward Hitchings Esq;
William Chapman Esq;
Mr. *Hawkins*
Mr. *Hutchins*
Mr. *Segar*
Mr. *Lowes*
Mr. *Collebe*
Mr. *Hill*
Mr. *Harford*
Mr. *Kingston*
Mr. *Mitchel*
Mr. *Reynolds*
Mr. *Wiltshire*
Mr. *Lewis*

STAFFORDSHIRE.
C. Fleetwood Esq;
Tho. Fitzherbert Esq;
Ralph Sneyd Esq;
Ralph Egerton Esq;
Tho. Burslem Esq;
Ralph Thickness Esq;
Craven Kinnersly Esq;
John Salt Esq;
E. Sneyd Esq;
John Coyney Esq;
William Hollins Esq;
James Wightwick Esq;
John Wryly Birch Esq;

—— *Wardle* Esq;
Mr. *Hadderton*
Mr. *Birch*
Mr. *Green*
Mr. *Richardson*
Mr. *Motterham*
Mr. *Hugeford*
Mr. *Ashly*
Mr. *Sills*
Mr. *Barber*
Mr. *Holmes*
Mr. *Tateham*
Mr. *Trubshaw*
Mr. *Ball*

SUFFOLK.
John Sheppard Esq;
John Barefoot Esq;
Richmond Garneys Esq;
Thomas Read Esq;
Valentine Munby Esq;
George Tasburg Esq;
Thomas Bransby Esq;
Capt. *Suckling*
Mr. *Naunton*
Mr. *Price*
Mr. *Nelson*
Mr. *Percival*

SURREY.
Charles Estwick Esq;
Tho. Neale Esq;
William Woodroffe Esq;
Joshua Smith Esq;
Mr. *North*
Mr. *Archer*
Mr. *Fish*
Mr. *Selby*

Mr.

Mr. *Bransby*
Mr. *Smith*
Mr. *Grande*
Mr. *Robinson*
Mr. *Watson*
Mr. *Thompson*
Mr. *Ireland*
Mr. *Proctor*
Mr. *Ovington*
Mr. *Smith*

SUSSEX.

Gawen Harris Nash Esq;
John Jewkes Esq;
Garton Orm Esq;
Richard Goodwin Esq;
John Newdigate Esq;
William Misford Esq;
Mr. *Lidgitter*
Mr. *Tench*
Mr. *Lickfold*

WARWICKSHIRE.

William Ebourn Esq;
William Neale Esq;
Tim. Stoughton Esq;
William Peyto Esq;
Bowyer Adderly Esq;
William Holbech Esq;
Booth Allestry Esq;
Jo. Webster Esq;
John Ludford Esq;
W. Green Esq;
Mr. *Welshman*
Mr. *Lane*
Mr. *Weal*
Mr. *Bowyer*
Mr. *Machin*

Mr. *Coles*
Mr. *Bradly*
Mr. *Bradly*
Mr. *French*

WESTMORELAND.

Robert Honeywood Esq;
Thomas Sheppard Esq;
Lanc. Machell Esq;
Mr. *Singleton*

WILTS.

George Penruddock Esq;
Francis Kenton Esq;
Richard Whitehead Esq;
—— *Chapman* Esq;
Tho. Earl Esq;
Robert Thompson Esq;
Thomas Hasket Esq;
Thomas Kington Esq;
Ger. Sheppard Esq;
Mr. *Reading*
Mr. *Haward*
Mr. *Lucas*
Mr. *Westly* at the *George Inn* in *Salisbury*
Mr. *Read*

WORCESTERSHIRE.

Rowland Berkley Esq;
Fra. Dowdeswell Esq;
Edward Lechmere Esq;
Tho. Acton, jun. Esq;
Capt. *Tracey*

YORKSHIRE.

Rev. Dr. *Sisson*

Q 2   Rev.

Rev. Mr. *Beavoir*
Rev. Mr. *Gee*
Jo. Milbank Esq;
Hen. Fletcher Esq;
—— *Hutchinson* Esq;
Edward Thompson Esq;
Hen. Peirse Esq;
Thomas Robinson Esq;
Leo. Childers Esq;
Jo. Bright Esq;
Tho. Bright Esq;
Cuth. Routh Esq;
Geo. Toulson Esq;
Robert Pockley Esq;
William Metcalf Esq;
John Ramsden Esq;
Francis Appleyard Esq;
Cyril Arthington Esq;
Va. Huntington Esq;
William Wombwell Esq;
Charles Bathurst Esq;
G. Wentworth Esq;
Rob. Raikes Fulsthorpe Esq;
Chom. Turner Esq;
Leo. Thompson Esq;
—— *Wrey* Esq;
Lewis Elstob Esq;
Hen. Hitch Esq;
Medcalf Robinson Esq;
Tho. Hassel Esq;
W. Hustler Esq;
Wardell G. Westby Esq;
C. Headlam Esq;
John Bourchier Esq;
Sherman Rokesby Esq;
—— *Clarke* Esq;
James Cooke Esq;
John Rawlinson Esq;

Richard Lepton Esq;
Christ. Wilson Esq;
Wharton Wharton Esq;
—— *Millits* Esq;
—— *Robinson* Esq;
John Wastell Esq;
H. Wood Esq;
William Vavasour Esq;
Wm. Kitchinman Esq;
Jamis Pennyman Esq;
Benjamin Purchase Esq;
Thomas Frankland Esq;
—— *Robinson* Esq;
—— *Anderson* Esq;
Thomas Gascoigne Esq;
—— *Langley* Esq;
John York Esq;
John Brewster Esq;
Robert Mitford Esq;
Hugh Fawsit Esq;
George Hassel Esq;
John Bacchus Esq;
John Hutton Esq;
Christopher Ayscough Esq;
William Horton Esq;
William Aistabie Esq;
Edward Wormsley Esq;
Matthew Smoles Esq;
Philip Byerly Esq;
Stephen Crofts Esq;
Hugh Bethel Esq;
Charles Newby Esq;
John Wilkinson Esq;
Richard Horton Esq;
Henry Frankland Esq;
John Maynard Esq;
George Beane Esq;

John

John Pulleine Esq;
John Taylor Esq;
William Chamber Esq;
—— Hodges Esq;
—— Prissick Esq;
Metcalf Proctor Esq;
William Simpson Esq;
William Pinkney Esq;
Thomas Clarke Esq;
William Wight Esq;
Mr. Frith
Mr. Bates
Mr. Crofts
Mr. Rickaby
Mr. Inman
Mr. Lister
Mr. Davile
Mr. Calverly
Mr. Thwaites
Mr. Ibetson
Mr. Mitchel
Mr. Greham
Mr. Watson
Mr. Backhouse
Mr. Marshal
Mr. Wyril
Mr. Johnson
Mr. Cosins
Mr. Bromhead
Mr. Brown
Mr. Smith
Mr. Clarke
Mr. Cowling
Mr. King
Mr. Hutton
Mr. Lowther
Mr. Fisher
Mr. Welbank
Mr. Stafford

Dr. Shaw
Mr. Ellis
Mr. Hammond
Mr. Redshaw
Mr. Boyes
Capt. Clough
Mr. Watson
Mr. Jawsey
Mr. Coats
Mr. Chapman
Mr. Smirke
Mr. Smith
Mr. Mason
Mr. Stavely
Mr. Proctor
Mr. Martin
Mr. Errat
Mr. Jackson
Mr. Barber
Mr. Waugh
Mr. Hardesty

SCOTLAND.
William Erskine Esq;
Samuel Berrisford Merriot Esq;
Mr. Thompson
Mr. Morgan

WALES.

CAERNARVANSHIRE.
William Wynn Esq;

DENBIGHSHIRE.
Watkin-Williams Wynn Esq;
Robert Williams Esq;
Q 3   Rob.

Rob. Middylton Esq;
Tho. Puleston Esq;
Aquila Wyke Esq;
Philip Egerton Esq;
Heath Lloyd Esq;
Enb. Lloyd Esq;
Mr. Porter.

FLINTSHIRE.
Richard Williams Esq;
Thomas Eyton Esq;
John Wynn Esq;
John Wynn, jun. Esq;

MONTGOMERYSHIRE.
Edward Williams Esq;

PEMBROKESHIRE.
John Phillips Esq;
John Barlow Esq;
Ed. Hen. Edwards Esq;

Mr. Thomas Errat
Mr. John Craggs
Mr. Fra. Law
Mr. Thomas Brice.
Mr. Ed. Smith.
Mr. George Oliver
Mr. William Grey
Mr. Thomas Welsh
Mr. Robert Bee
Mr. Samuel Stevenson
Mr. Thomas Hahns
Mr. William Oldham
Mr. Jo. Nose
Mr. Tho. Bradly
Mr. Thomas Hawkins
Mr. Fra. Beeland

Mr. Reyn. Higgins
Mr. Henry Chaplin
Mr. Char. Jackson
Mr. John Wilkins
Mr. Robert Bruce
Mr. Thomas Barret
Mr. William Hewbrew
Mr. William Headly
Mr. James Larkin
Mr. Thomas Miller
Mr. Robert Watts
Mr. Jo. Bennet
Mr. Richard Thompson
Mr. Rob. Otter
Mr. Sim. Clarke
Mr. William Simkins
Mr. Jo. Cooper
Mr. Richard Hayes
Mr. William Headly, jun.
Mr. John Harrison
Mr. Richard March
Mr. Joseph Errat
Mr. Austin Lidbury
Mr. George Tusing
Mr. Thomas Wilson
Mr. Thomas Dean
Mr. John South
Mr. Philip Osbaldston
Mr. Richard Griffith
Mr. Sam. Haraps
Mr. William Scarf
Mr. Thomas Bilison
Mr. Noble
Mr. Richard Ball
Mr. Hart
Mr. Richard Thompson
Mr. John Ducker
Mr. Huggart

Mr.

Mr. Thomas Williamson
Mr. John Carter
Mr. John Sleight
Mr. George Bowles
Mr. James Groves
Mr. Richard Reve
Mr. Robert Noy
Mr. Richard Ball
Mr. John Benson
Mr. Thomas Abbot
Mr. Ed. Chapman
Mr. Beacon
Mr. W. Grey
Mr. W. Huggart
Mr. Jos. Smith.
Mr. Tho. Orrington
Mr. Geo. Bowes
Mr. Ja. Benson
Mr. Val. Tree
Mr. Rich. Gates
Mr. Tho. Watson
Mr. Jos. Nell
Mr. Geo. Green.
Mr. W. Obrien.

Mr. W. Crowder
Mr. Rich. Milburn
Mr. Barlow
Mr. Benny
Mr. James Cooke
Mr. ——— Morgan
Mr. Matcham Timms
Mr. Peter Grandee
Mr. James Blackburn
Mr. William Banister
Mr. Stephen Dodd
Mr. James Well
Mr. Bennet Barber
Mr. Richard Dyer
Mr. Thomas Turner
Mr. William Brion
Mr. Ed. Ellis
Mr. Christopher Treves
Mr. David Place
Mr. King Vickers
Mr. George Green
Mr. Thomas Cope
Mr. Hugh Comley.

Rr

An ALPHABETICAL LIST of the Places of Sport mention'd in the foregoing Book.

F I N I S.

CPSIA information can be obtained
at www.ICGtesting.com
Printed in the USA
BVOW04s1013060917

494113BV00010B/230/P